How Firm A Foundation

Historic Houses of Grey County

by
Ruth Cathcart
Photography by Willy Waterton

Drawings by Bert de Graaf

THE RED HOUSE PRESS

CANADIAN CATALOGUING IN PUBLICATION DATA

Cathcart, Ruth, 1932-
How firm a foundation : historic houses of Grey County

Includes bibliographical references.
ISBN 0-9681375-0-4

1. Historic buildings–Ontario–Grey (County)
2. Architecture, Domestic–Ontario–Grey (County)–History. 3. Grey (Ont. : County)–Buildings, structures, etc. I. Title.

NA7242.05C37 1996 971.3'18 C96-900806-6

Published by The Red House Press, Box 927, Wiarton, Ontario N0H 2T0
Phone (519) 534-2439 Fax (519) 534-3228

Typeset & Printed by Stan Brown Printers Ltd., Owen Sound, Ontario

Front Cover: The Cleland/Clarke House, Meaford, Ontario
Back Cover: The Patrick Kelly House, Sullivan Township, Ontario

Dedication

For my husband Murray, and for my friend Donna Wickham, who took pity on me during the harsh winter of 1993-1994 and took over the driving, up and down the concessions and sideroads of Grey and Bruce Counties, in our quest for historic houses.

INSCRIPTION

"He builded better than he knew; The concious stone to beauty grew."

Ralph Waldo Emerson

Table Of Contents

ACKNOWLEDGEMENTS

Owners and former owners of the properties described in this book were eager to share their information with me. Their letters, telephone calls, and invitations to visit, indicated to me their love and appreciation of the houses in their possession. Written family histories, family trees and vintage photographs were lent to me. I am grateful for their assistance.

They are: Mr. & Mrs. Kenneth Rae, Alena Graham, J. McWilliam, Guido & Hilda Van den Daele, David & Sandra Walton-Ball, John Landon, Susan Lewis, Lorne Johnson, Chris Irvine, Katie Van Elphen, Nan Maitland, Ida Piplack, Charles McPhatter, John Dales, Ronald Jones, Grace Glass, T.J. Van Dam, Alison McRonald, Ruth Kritsch, Lois Legge, Donna King, Douglas Beckett, Gabrielle Robertson, Margaret Sieling, Carole Ann Parker, Laura Hill, Brenda Keyes, James Baskerville, Carole Parker, Donna Beckett, William Van Halem, Brenda Fowler, Cecil Barber, F. M. Springvail, Faye Bayly, James Armstrong, Alice C. Heard, Suzanne Bate, Jennie Burg, Albert McInnis, Douglas & Margaret Gray, Helen Harpley, Garry Swayze, Josephine Hebert, Robert Lyons, Lynne Beaton, Richard Camsell, Grant May, Phyllis Armstrong, Dennis Longpre, Lois Henry, Timothy Bardeau, Jacob Friesen, Frances McIvor, Peter Clarke, Ross Leibold, Eric Fischer, Roy Fischer, Shirley Hartley, Mary Harrison, Glen Norman, E. Cook, Donald Powers, Jimmy Brunow, Ross Drummond, T.J. Heatherington, J. Turner, Carol & Wayne Lee, Sheilah Fletch, Betty Lewin, Mary Cohen, Jaffray & Betty Rutherford, Kay Morrison, Ina Piplack, Viola Bothwell, Charles Turner, Rita Eagles, Don Cianci, Helga Kessler.

Other individuals whose combined knowledge of local history is impressive were generous in sharing it. They are: Dorothy Telford, Carol McKee, Barry More, Bert Morrison, Doug Wood, Paula Niall, Millie Hubbert, Tom Firth, Josephine Feairs and Andrew Armitage.

Sandy Tomlin, coordinator of Owen Sound LACAC (Local Architectural Conservation Advisory Committee) made research material available to me and wrote a letter asking the Land Registry Office to permit me to search land titles at no cost. Peter Hillyer, a free lance title searcher, did his best to teach me how to interpret those complex documents.

Finally, professional staff at three institutions in this area more than fulfilled their responsibilities to the researcher. Joan Hyslop at the Grey-Owen Sound Museum is the model archivist. Historical material in the museum collection is at her fingertips. Andrew Armitage, chief librarian, and his staff at the Owen Sound and North Grey Union Public Library run a tight ship and a lovely and serene place in which to work. The Local History Collection there is a community treasure. Finally, the Land Registry Office of Grey County agreed to allow me to search land titles free of charge and tolerated my barging around their space week after week.

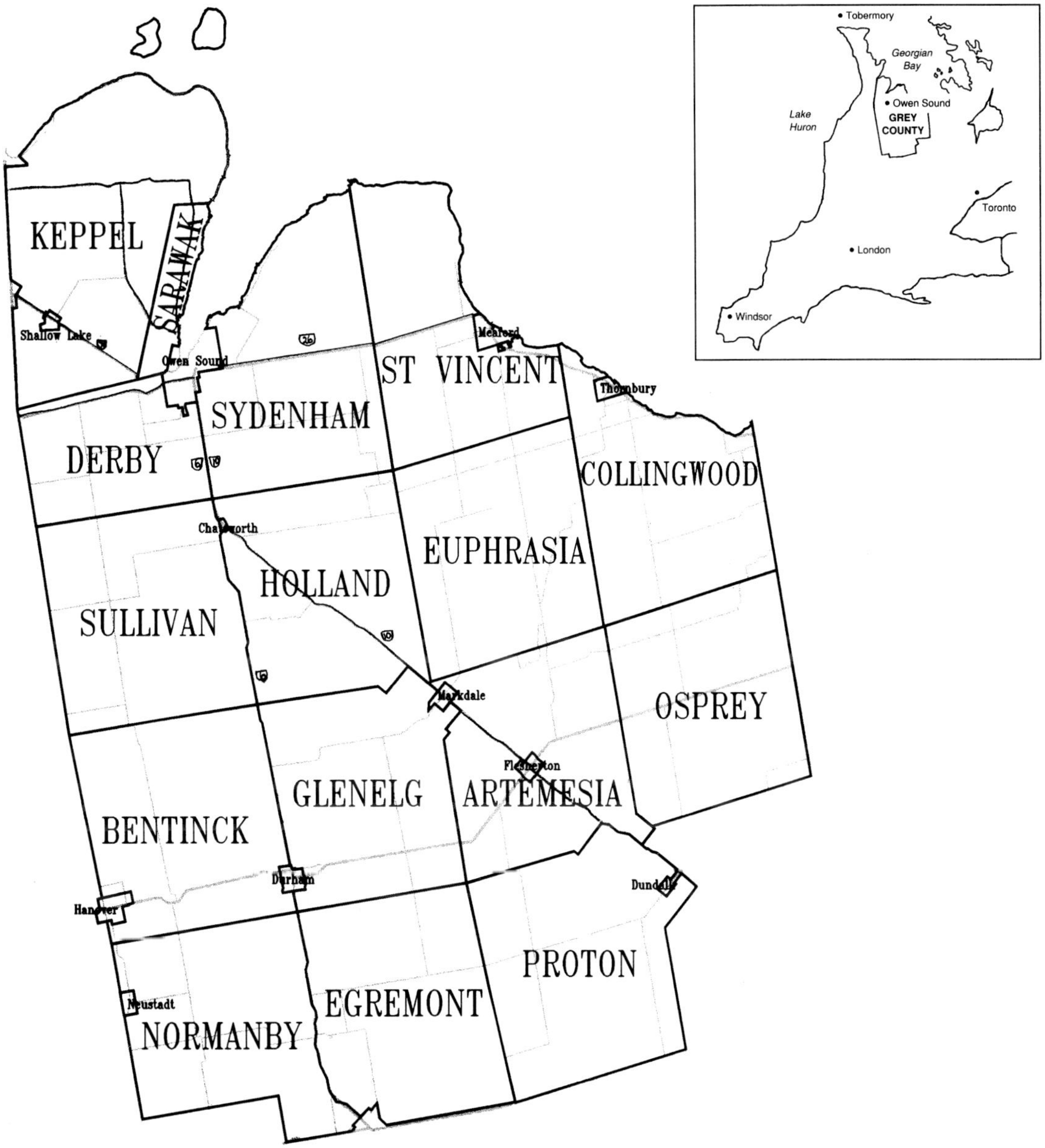
KEPPEL
SARAWAK
Shallow Lake
Owen Sound
Meaford
ST VINCENT
Thornbury
SYDENHAM
DERBY
COLLINGWOOD
Chatsworth
EUPHRASIA
HOLLAND
SULLIVAN
Markdale
OSPREY
Flesherton
GLENELG
ARTEMESIA
BENTINCK
Durham
Hanover
Dundalk
PROTON
Neustadt
EGREMONT
NORMANBY
Tobermory
Georgian Bay
Lake Huron
Owen Sound
GREY COUNTY
Toronto
London
Windsor

GREY COUNTY

INTRODUCTION

"All architecture reveals the application of human ingenuity to the satisfaction of human needs. And among those needs are not only shelter, warmth and accommodation but also the needs, felt at every moment in every part of the world in endless different ways, for something more profound, evocative and universal, for beauty, for permanence, for immortality."

Patrick Nuttgens — *The Story of Architecture*
Phaidon Press Ltd., London. 1983. p.280

This book reflects a vital interest in domestic architecture which grew, as the work progressed, into a fascination with the lives of those who built and inhabited their pioneer homes. The settlers came to this region of Canada to escape the catastrophes of war, famine, bondage to inhumane landlords and social systems which kept them in penury. They came mainly from the British Isles and Germany.

Others, many fewer in number, were members of the educated classes in the old countries who saw, in the new world, the opportunity to expand their lives, to construct a freer and more productive lifestyle. These upper class immigrants soon assumed positions of authority such as Sheriff, Registrar of Lands or Member of Parliament in their communities. They built mills, became merchants, opened quarries and brickyards. And many built their personal fortunes by speculating in land.

Often the first generation of our Grey County pioneers settled in the southern parts of Upper Canada in order to generate enough savings with which to migrate farther north and to wait for the roads which would open up the country. Other settlers arrived directly from the British Isles or from continental Europe.

They came to Grey County in the second half of the nineteenth century either over water via Lake

Simcoe and Georgian Bay or over land via the colonization roads which were opened around 1850. The Toronto-Sydenham Road (now Highway 10) provided a more direct connection between Toronto and Sydenham (Owen Sound). The Garafraxa Road (now Highway 6) ran north from Arthur to the mouth of the Sydenham River. And the Durham Road (now Highway 4 & 9) ran from east to west from Priceville to Kincardine. The Crown allocated free fifty-acre lots along these routes subject to the performance of settlement duties. Alternate fifty-acre lots were left available to be sold later to the settlers on the free lots, to complete the usual one hundred-acre estate.

Settlement duties varied from area to area but usually consisted of building a dwelling of a certain size within the first year and occupying it for a fixed period. The land was to be cleared at the rate of about five acres per year, planted and fenced. After completing his settlement duties the settler's grant of land was confirmed. However it may not have been Patented immediately. Land sometimes passed through many hands by sale or inheritance before the Patent was issued — perhaps decades after the original grant.

The first shelter was often a crude log shanty with a shed roof. The chinks between the logs were stuffed with splints, moss or clay. The roof was made of tree bark and the door of planks. If there were a window it might have been faced with oiled paper. As soon as possible this shelter was replaced by a more substantial log house of perhaps twenty by thirty feet with or without an upper half-storey. It provided a kitchen and two bedrooms, or a kitchen, a parlour and a bedroom downstairs and several bedrooms upstairs. Half storeys provided the needed accommodation for large pioneer families and were not taxable.

Many of these logs houses in Grey County are still standing. They have been covered over by wood, brick or stone and more recently by insulbrick, aluminum or vinyl, for warmth and a more up-to-date appearance. They have usually been enlarged by the addition of a "working tail" which consisted of a summer kitchen or a wood shed or a drive shed or any combination of the above.

A typical log house

The log house was succeeded by a frame, brick or stone version of much the same style, which is commonly known as "Ontario Gothic." It is a rectangular structure with the front facade in the long axis. A centre front entrance is flanked by symmetrically placed windows. Above the entrance a peaked gable contains a window. A pitched roof with gable ends and an interior brick chimney complete the picture of a house which is the hallmark of Grey County domestic architecture. It is a pragmatic adaptation of the "ancestral small Renaissance house of western Europe" described by Marion Macrae and Anthony Adamson in their book, *The Ancestral Roof — Domestic Architecture In Upper Canada* (page 226). It was built to suit our climate, the availability of local materials and the skills of our craftsmen.

Ontario Gothic – The generic Grey County House

Other more sophisticated architectural styles in their vernacular forms (not generated by a professional architect but reflecting popular practice) soon began to appear in Grey County. These styles embodied the ideas brought from the old countries by colonists and to some extent from ideas culled from English and American style books. In the first one or two decades of settlement, aside from the generic "Ontario Gothic," the severely rational Georgian style was most common. But soon the picturesque styles of the Gothic Revival and the Regency Cottage appeared, followed by the High Victorian styles of French Second Empire and Italianate.

The Georgian style of architecture is named for the English monarchs of the 18th and early 19th centuries. It centres around the idea of the beauty of symmetry and proportion. This idea came from Greek and Roman classicism which celebrated the rational — reason, order, decorum and repose over all else. The

Georgian house featured a central entrance, emphasized by a glazed transom and sidelights. Windows are isolated against a clean wall and are symmetrically placed. Quoins highlight the corners. A continuous cornice and sometimes a beltway to delineate the two storeys, stress the horizontal orientation of the two-storey building. Chimneys and flues receive great care and attention. Simplicity, wholeness and pristine clarity are further delineated by a hipped or gable-end roof. A firm relationship to the land gives the structure a feeling of stability and permanence.

Georgian

The Picturesque Movement in England grew out of love of natural scenery. Houses were viewed as an integral but subsidiary part of an overall scenic composition. This provided the justification for an eclectic approach to style. Importance was placed on irregular silhouette, varied planes and textures with resulting light and shadow, delicate detail and subtle colour. Architectural elements were verandahs, French and bay windows, roughcast walls, blocky or tall chimneys, wide bracketed eaves, bargeboard (gingerbread), chamfered corners, ornamental balconies, roof cresting and belvederes or roofwalks.

Gothic Revival became synonymous with the term, Picturesque. The main design element of this style in Grey County is irregularity of outline, achieved by the use of bay windows, ells and verandahs. Roofs are steeply pitched and multiple gables feature lacy bargeboard. Windows are protected by Tudor or Gothic labels.

Gothic Revival

The Ontario or Regency Cottage is characterized by a square floor plan with a centre hall. Its gently pitched, hipped roof sometimes contains an attic with sleeping quarters. It is low in mass and lends itself to almost any style of detailing — perhaps Greek in the pediment, Gothic in the bargeboard, or Second Empire in the cresting of the truncated roof.

The Ontario or Regency Cottage

High Victorianism in architecture manifested itself in two urban styles in this region. They are Italianate and French Second Empire.

The Italianate style, also referred to as the Tuscan or Bracketed style, derived from the villa architecture of Tuscany in Italy. It features round-headed windows (sometimes paired), watchtowers (sometimes balconied) and wide eaves with brackets. In this region the style is almost always confined to urban areas. It was used as vehicle to express wealth, sophistication and dignity.

Italianate

The Second Empire style (Napoleon Bonaparte founded the First Empire) originated in Paris in the 1840's. Napoleon 111 and Georges-Eugene Haussmann, who was Prefect of the Seine, carried out the biggest urban renewal project the world had ever seen in order to provide visual unity to the city. The style was synonymous with the mansard roof, named for the seventeenth century French architect, François Mansart. The roof slopes up in two degrees on all four sides, the initial slope being steeper. It was designed to provide more space in the upper storey. Often iron cresting was applied to the roof to soften the abrupt finish of the roofline as seen from the street. This style was introduced into Ontario at about the time of Confederation and into Grey County only a few years later.

Second Empire

Finally, in a discussion of the architectural styles popular in Grey County in the early days, it must be pointed out that there was considerable mixing and matching of stylistic details. Few builders restricted themselves to pure expressions of a recognizable style. Trained architects were scarce. And, especially as the Victorian age matured, there were so many ideas to choose from coupled with a middle-class inclination to display wealth that decoration was sometimes piled upon decoration.

In the towns and villages of Grey County the earliest houses are often found hidden in mature stands of Norway Spruce. In the countryside early houses are situated at the end of long lanes — far back from the local road — because mobility was not the prime factor it is today. Then, horses pulling cutters or wagons could negotiate snowy or muddy lanes more effectively than can the automobile in today's world. Also, site was carefully considered in the countryside. Barns and sheds were located in reference to the house and the composite farmstead formed a working unit that is, typically, a picturesque addition to the landscape.

The building materials for our early houses were abundant and, in some cases, free of cost. Logs were in oversupply. Settlers felled the timber on their lots not only for their own purposes but also for sale to the sawmills springing up throughout the countryside. Stone was found on many homesteads and used in the fieldstone or rubble masonry of the houses. Limestone quarries supplied sawn or squared stone for ashlar masonry. Almost every town or village had a brickyard. These natural materials age to a patina which cannot be matched by modern materials such as cement brick, aluminum or vinyl. In the early days building materials were not used as cladding, with the exception sometimes of brick, but as structural material. Solid stone and double or triple brick walls can exceed three feet in width.

It is important to describe the criteria used in the choice of the houses described in this volume. Although every effort was made to locate all of the early houses of Grey county, inevitably some will have been missed. Of those recorded many were not considered for inclusion because they did not fit the following criteria.

The most obvious criterion is that of age. The older the house the more interest it holds for the historian and the more important is its existence today within the community.

The second criterion has to do with aesthetics. Does the house please the eye? Is it well-sited? Are the stylistic details consistent, interesting, unique? Is the craftsmanship high in quality?

The third criterion poses the most difficulty. It is authenticity. Old houses are bound to change, to evolve over the decades to meet the needs of new owners. Services such as plumbing and heating are updated as technology grows. More space is need as families enlarge. Windows, verandahs and roofs must be replaced. Some old houses are admirably suited to conversion to apartments or office space. The houses chosen for inclusion in this volume are those which, in spite of their evolution, have preserved their original "look." These houses have maintained their integrity, their charm, their interest, their history. Thankfully, the preservation movement in architecture is teaching us that old houses must be protected, not only for aesthetic and historical reasons but because they have intrinsic economic value which can be greatly reduced if unsympathetic practices are used in their evolution.

Such unsympathetic changes to old houses include recladding the structure with modern materials, punching a picture window or sliding glass doors through the front facade, tearing down the chimneys or replacing an aging verandah with a modern deck. Many such depredations continue to occur despite the good work in educating the public done by local LACAC groups (Local Architectural Conservation Advisory Committees). But an interesting phenomenon is also occurring in which city dwellers from elsewhere and some local people are buying our historic houses for first or second homes. They proceed to carefully rehabilitate these structures which otherwise would certainly have been lost to us.

The fourth criterion is historical relevance. What does the house tell us about the lives of the people who built it, particularly the lives of prominent historical figures? By the way, the accepted custom of naming a house after the then head of the family in no way denigrates or ignores the huge contribution made by his wife and children to pioneer family life.

Criterion number five is photographability. Some early houses are so obscured by closely planted and overgrown trees and shrubs that they are impossible to photograph.

Finally, an effort was made to distribute the chosen houses over all of the townships of Grey County and to demonstrate ethnic-based differences in construction and design.

There is almost no literature on the subject of the early houses in the regions north of the southern corridor of Ontario. This volume hopes to fill that gap. Although the hundred or so houses described here are all found in Grey County, they are typical of those found in the other counties of south-central and central Ontario. They form a collection of the common styles of domestic architecture built of typical materials found over a wide area.

The historic houses of this region stand as testimony to the sturdy and industrious character of the people who built them and lived in them. Above all, they demonstrate their inhabitants' dreams for permanence and grace in the new land.

ARTEMESIA TOWNSHIP

"The Brick" c.1882

Artemesia Township S Pt Lot 1 Con 7

IMAGINE YOURSELF DRIVING down a sideroad in an area which can truly be described as "the backwoods." Suddenly, rising to meet you is a massive two-storey brick house (aptly named) complete with the design vocabulary of High Victorian architecture. The roof is hipped, the four tall brick chimneys have projecting top courses, double brackets emphasize the wide eaves, a small front gable/pediment highlights an attic oculus, bay windows are crested with lacy wrought iron, and a projecting entrance foyer is highlighted by a handsome round-topped double door.

The house was built on thirteen acres fronting on Irish Lake; so-called because the early settlers there were mainly Irish Catholics. Land Registry records show that the original forty-four acre lot was granted by the Crown to one Michael Morgan in 1868. The Roman Catholic Diocese of Hamilton bought the parcel on the lake and built the house under the supervision of Father Patrick Joseph Cassin. Subsequent priests serving the community were Father John J. Feeney and Father Richard Maloney.

THE JONATHON HICKLING HOUSE C.1875

Artemesia Township Lot 39 Con 8

JONATHON HICKLING AND his wife, Elizabeth, bought this one hundred and ninety-nine acre property for $1200 in 1873 from Alexander Neilson who had received it as a free grant from the Crown in 1867. The carefully maintained log house on the property was perhaps Neilson's homestead. The stone house is thought to have been built by Hickling. The stone driving shed at the rear has been reduced to a walled garden.

It is a generic house of Georgian classicism with its firm relationship to the land and its symmetry. What sets this house apart from so many early stone houses in this region is the checkerboard effect of the stonework. The builder has carefully composed his cut fieldstones in a regular pattern of light and dark. Even the segmental stones over the windows and the door of the facade alternate between light and dark. The modest doorway is slightly recessed and boasts a glass transom to light the centre hall. An anchor board has been set into the stonework a couple of feet above the window tops for the purpose of attaching a verandah to two sides of the structure. It is not known if such a verandah ever existed.

THE WILLIAM WRIGHT HOUSE C.1875

Artemesia Township Lot 136-137 Con 3 WTSR

THIS COMMANDING BRICK and stone house stands on a slight rise of land looking eastward. It is sheltered from the prevailing westerly winds by the bank into which the house is built and the huge Norway Spruce planted there long ago. The second-floor rear actually opens to the outside just three steps above ground level. The sides of the main floor and the lower portion of the back of the house are constructed of stone. The remainder of the house is solid brick, three bricks thick.

A two-and-a-half-storey central gable house, its most interesting features are the pointed arched window, the closed second-floor porch built in 1928, set into the verandah roof built in 1909, and the entrance lit by transom and sidelights. The application of Gothic detail; gable bargeboard and finial, pointed window, and lacy verandah brackets, on an otherwise Georgian body, gives the house a spirit of liveliness.

Thomas Racey settled here in 1852, on land granted by the Crown. In 1867 the property was sold for back taxes by the Sheriff of Grey County to William Wright who had come to Artemesia in about 1854. He married Margaret Gillespie in 1856, and they raised ten children. Their youngest son, John E. Wright came into possession of the farm in 1901. By 1913 the George Cairns family had bought the property. A son, William F. Cairns acquired it in 1946 and his descendants retain ownership to this day.

THE JOHN WESLEY ARMSTRONG HOUSE c.1880

Artemesia Township Pt Lot 155 Con 2 ETSR

IN 1855 WILLIAM GOOD received the Patent from the Crown for Lot 155 and in 1856 he acquired the adjoining Lot 154 for fifty cents an acre. Twenty years later the executors of his estate sold the property to J. W. Armstrong, who later became a well-known citizen of the town of Flesherton. On page 313 of *Split Rail Country — A History of Artemesia Township,* we are told that Armstrong was the first teacher at Section #4 Victoria Corners School. He held a second-class Teaching Certificate and received a yearly salary of £30.

The central gable of this vernacular house permits a window to light the upper floor and gives the house an air of distinction, similar in effect to a classical pediment in a two-storey house. The gable is ornamented with bargeboard tracery and the verandah roof with a row of spindles and more tracery. The solid red brick construction of the house is also ornamented with buff brick in a curious but pleasant quoining effect at the corners, buff brick window heads, and a chain link design which runs around the house just above the level of the verandah roof.

THE WATSON HOUSE c.1900

Village of Priceville   Plan 10 Pt lot 2 & 3   Kinross Street South, Priceville, ON N0C 1K0

PRICEVILLE IS AN ENCHANTING village in the valley of the Saugeen River. Its first settlers were American Blacks who, along with other United Empire Loyalists, came north after the American Revolution of 1770. Their leader was a gentleman farmer from Alabama whose name was Colonel Price. He helped to survey the village which was named after him. As Loyalists they were given grants of land along the Old Durham Road. Their church was a log building with a graveyard nearby. According to *Priceville And Its Roots (Routes)*, page 2, that graveyard had been plowed up for potatoes in 1930 and the gravestones smashed and concealed in a rock pile. In 1990 a monument was dedicated here in the presence of the Lieutenant Governor of Ontario, Lincoln Alexander, so that we should not forget these first settlers.

British immigrants, predominantly Scots, began to arrive about 1850. Saw and grist mills were built on the Saugeen River. The town prospered until, at the turn of the century, there were five churches, five hotels and half a dozen general stores. Today's Priceville has shrunk in population but has lost none of its special charm.

The brickwork in this house is what sets it apart. A plain rectangular structure is given life by the use of red and black brick patterning in a buff brick body. The pattern in the front gable is reminiscent of the hex signs which decorate many barns in this region.

BENTINCK TOWNSHIP

STILLMEADOW ACRES c.1865

Bentinck Township Con 1 WGR Pt. Div. 1 Lot 28 Part 3 Ref Plan 17R1125 (Douglas St. W. Town of Durham)

THIS REGENCY COTTAGE with its sharply rising hipped roof is a pleasing stylistic mix of the strict classical mode and the reinterpretation of the Gothic mode in the second half of the nineteenth century. To the symmetry of the design is added decorative brickwork, a gable centred by a pointed arch window and large three-sided front bays topped with three-sided roofs.

Land Registry records show that the Crown granted this property to a John Brownslow in 1855. Because it was located at the southern edge of the town of Durham it was soon divided into building lots and the identity of the person(s) who conceived it is lost in the mists of time.

The Robertson House c.1875

Bentinck Township Pt Lot 4 Con 13

FRIENDS, HUGH BARTON and John Robertson, came from Scotland together in 1858 and eventually took up adjoining properties in Bentinck Township. They were stone cutters who had worked on Brock's Monument in Queenston for three and a half years before coming to Grey County. Robertson cut the stone and built his own house in the early 1870's and according to *A History of Bentinck Township* (page 282), died of silicosis in 1876.

His house is beautifully made. Cut stone of regular size is carefully coursed — larger stones in the lower ranks to smaller ones in the upper ranks. The openings are surrounded by smoothly dressed stone slabs. Chimneys at either end of the gable roof are constructed of the same regular stonework. The house was unadorned until recently when the verandah was added; depending on simplicity and expert masonry for its strong presence.

Poplar Hill – The Richard Backhouse House c.1860

Bentinck Township Lot 70 Con 3 WGR

THE FIRST STRUCTURE to be built on this property was a log shanty erected in 1857 by Richard Backhouse. This stone house was said to have been built in 1860 and the Crown deed to the land is dated 1868. Backhouse named his farm "Poplar Hill" after the Lombardy Poplars he had imported from England and planted in 1868.

Methodist services, in which Mrs. Backhouse led the singing, were held in the kitchen of the stone house. She also worked as a midwife and nurse in the community. She and Richard raised four girls and one boy. When their son John, married Mary Ann Adlam in 1876 a frame house was built for them on the property. According to family tradition, when the barn was built in 1894 their eight year old daughter baked all the pies for the barn raising. Since 1927 the farm has been held in the name of McRonald.

There was a small Indian Band nearby whose members proved to be good neighbours to the Backhouses. As an example; one winter when one of their daughters injured her ankle, Indian neighbours took her to and from school in a sled.

Such are the family stories connected with a modest rubble-stone house built in the generic style of the time — Georgian. A roof with gable ends, symmetrically placed openings, internal chimneys and a tail behind for summer kitchen and woodshed are typical. Red brick quoins and window heads add colour and character to this historic house.

Photo by Ruth Cathcart

TOWN OF CLARKSBURG

GRAPE GRANGE (MARSH HOMESTEAD) C.1865

Clarksburg Collingwood Township. Pt Lot 57 Plan 562

WILLIAM JABEZ MARSH, the founder of Clarksburg, arrived there in 1861. He had first settled in Thornbury as a merchant in 1858. His Clarksburg property comprised almost four hundred acres on the 9th and 10th concessions of Collingwood Township. He sold some of this land, along the Beaver River, to a William Clark from the United States who built woolen and grist mills — hence the name Clarksburg. Collingwood Township assessment rolls for 1872 note that Marsh's property was valued at $4,430, that there were four persons in the family and that they owned twenty cattle, thirty-three sheep, thirteen hogs and six horses. This was a considerable estate in 1872 in Collingwood Township. Nan Maitland, a direct descendant of William J. Marsh to the fourth generation, runs the house presently as a Bed & Breakfast establishment.

This, the oldest house in the village, was built of logs. It was later clapboarded and then veneered with brick at which time the conservatory and bay windows were probably added. The pitched roof of this "Ontario cottage" is interrupted by a very large front gable featuring a finial and a circular attic ventilator. Three towering black walnut trees in the lawn were planted by William Jabez Marsh assisted by his son, Charles.

The Doctor's House c.1875

Clarksburg Lot 15 Marsh St. E. Plan 562

Dr. R. H. Hunt arrived in Clarksburg in 1869 and a few years later had this substantial two-storey brick house built to accommodate his family and his office. He practiced in this lovely town until his death in 1929. The house has continued to provide living and office space for many of the years since. The present incumbent is a physician.

Its brickwork is patterned in the usual way. Lintels, quoins and frieze are emphasized by the use of buff brick against the red brick walls. An interesting variation is found in the way the frieze pattern accommodates double roof brackets. The second storey balcony-porch roof echoes the roof of the house and reinforces the pleasing symmetry of the whole structure.

COLLINGWOOD TOWNSHIP

The Adam Barr Homestead c.1870

Collingwood Township Lot 1 Con 1

THIS UNFORGETTABLE LITTLE frame house is situated in the Pretty River Valley in Collingwood Township. In the book, *"An Illustrated History of Collingwood Township,"* page 186, published in 1979, this description of the valley gives us a feeling for its loveliness:

"At the very southeastern end of the township, lies a world of its own in a valley that falls steeply on three sides to a sparkling stream at the bottom that winds among the trees hidden from view. This is the valley of the Pretty River. The rim of hills circles it on the south, west and north and only on the eastern side lies open and descends to the flats of Nottawasaga. Within the valley itself there are steep hills and valleys, either bald and windswept from the years when sheep grazed over them, or covered in dense maple forest which, to many travelers first entering the valley from the ridge four hundred feet above the stream at the bottom, is a sight too beautiful to forget."

Adam Barr, born in 1826, came to this country from Paisley, Scotland and is listed in the first Collingwood census of 1851. His wife was Anne, the daughter of Donald Currie, an early settler in Nottawasaga. The 1872 census shows that the Barr establishment had grown to include seven children, twelve cattle, seven sheep, twenty hogs and three horses. By 1886 the assessed value of the 200 acre farm was $3200, taxed at the rate of $37.53.

The Scottish community in the Pretty River Valley remained distinct and separate from the rest of the township - separated not only by geography but by inclination. These Scots were an independent tribe! The first school, a union school for three townships, was built on Adam Barr's farm in 1859. It has been described as being of log construction with a log house for the teacher, Malcolm Smith.

One of the saddest stories ever told in this region is the story of the death of one of Adam Barr's daughters. She was a little thing who had a pet squirrel. It bit her one day as she was playing with it. She was infected with rabies and to still her terrible suffering, for which there was no help, her parents smothered her with a pillow.

This plain, white frame house with green trim has much to say to us. Its people had a vision of a new and better life in a new place. For this vision they struggled and wept. They worked extremely hard to support themselves and to create a community. We are humble in their remembered presence.

The Barclay House and Camperdown Post Office c.1885

Collingwood Township Pt. Lt. 27 Con 7

JAMES BARCLAY'S LARGE, roughcast, two-storey house served as his home and a post office from 1887 until 1964. It is situated on what was the Lake Shore Road and railway line and what is now Highway 26 between the cities of Collingwood and Owen Sound. After his father's death in 1924 James Barclay Jr. continued the family vocation of postmaster for another forty years.

A photograph published in *An Illustrated History of Collingwood Township,* 1979, page 94, shows James Barclay Jr. hanging a mail sack on a pole beside the train track where a trainman would snatch it as the train passed.

Artist Robert C. Kemp, in his book, *Grey, Bruce, Simcoe Counties, Some of Its Places and Faces,* has included this sensitive portrait of James Barclay Jr. and his house.

The Wright House c.1873

Collingwood Township Pt. Lot 23 Con 8

Early houses of patterned brick are common in Grey and Bruce Counties. This house is an exceptionally fine example. Buff brick has been used in a pattern to relieve the monotony of the red brick walls, a design idea applied to some Georgian manor houses in England. The English derived the idea from medieval Italian architecture. Contrasting patterns surround the windows and the entrance, and constitute raised quoins and an elegant frieze under the roof. This generic "Ontario" cottage is further enhanced by Gothic Revival tracery bargeboard with a finial in the peak of the front gable and by the generosity and grace of its front entrance. Again, as is common, the front door is a "ritual" door. The main entrance is tucked in between the summer kitchen and the main house where it is protected from the weather. At one time a verandah graced the front elevation.

Richard Wright, born in 1825 in Ireland, acquired the north half of lot 23, Concession 8 in the 1850's. By 1873 its assessed value was $2400. Little more is known of the family which had the will and the means to build such a pleasing and well-balanced solid brick house.

THE BROWNLEE HOUSE C.1885

Collingwood Township Pt. Lot 18 Con 8

THREE GABLES AND three chimneys enliven the design of the long front elevation of this Gothic-Revival house. The larger, centre gable is further differentiated by twin windows upstairs and a bay window below. On either side of the bay window are awning-roofed verandahs supported by slender three-piece Gothic columns. This brick house painted white with slate-coloured roofs and trim is a pleasure to look upon. It is substantial yet picturesque; an accomplished example of the vernacular in Ontario domestic architecture.

Robert Brownlee received title to this lot in 1862. In 1868 he willed the south half of his two hundred acres to his cousin, James Brownlee and the north half to Jane Brownlee. James Brownlee, born in 1832, had a family of six children one of whom, Frank, continued on the farm raising Clydesdales and becoming a veterinarian. His son Russell, represented the next generation on the land and now Clifford Brownlee, the fourth generation, continues the tradition.

Pinnacle Rock Farm c.1875

Collingwood Township N Pt Lot 7 Con 12

Southern portions of Collingwood Township are wildly beautiful. The south western area in which this house is located is characterized by hardwood forests interspersed with cedar swamps and traversed by Kolapore Creek. The aboriginal people surrendered this territory (now Collingwood and St. Vincent Townships) in a treaty made in 1818. *An Illustrated History of Collingwood Township,* page 29, reads: "There is not a single recorded instance of resentment or antagonism by the Indian people to any Collingwood Township settler, even when the maple sugar groves and hunting forests were cut down, the game and fishing taken from them, their wandering freedom curtailed."

As was usual in these "back" townships, the land was granted to members of the Family Compact, to people of some wealth and influence. Very few of them (British officers, children of the United Empire Loyalists and any man who joined the militia in preparation for the war of 1812) had any interest in becoming pioneer bush farmers and the land passed into the hands of speculators to be sold and resold. The ownership history of the lot on which this house stands illustrates this process. It was granted in 1837 to a Pamela Wiltse, of whom we have no personal record, and was promptly sold in that year and resold in the following year with the price rising steadily. In 1853 it went to James Paul and appears to have remained in the ownership of that family for at least twenty-five years.

The house is a simple two-story cube topped by the usual hipped roof. It presents a symmetrical facade of three bays on the main floor with an unusual placement of the three windows on the second floor. Although the new cladding is not of wood, the house is attractive and is framed by mature trees. It is sited on a high ridge with magnificent views from the rear.

Photo by Ruth Cathcart

DERBY TOWNSHIP

THE ALEXANDER FLEMING HOUSE 1864

Derby Township Lots 9 & 10 Con 6 – now moved to Leith in Sydenham Township

ALEXANDER (1799-1869) AND Jean Stewart Fleming (1803-1888) came from Perthshire, Scotland to Canada with their eight children in 1843. The ninth was born three days after their arrival in Vaughn Township. Alexander and his sons were to clear fifty acres of land at five dollars an acre for the local squire, William Richard Graham, in order to earn enough money to buy land of their own. In 1847 Alexander Fleming was able to buy four hundred acres from the Crown in Derby Township for the equivalent of $2.00 an acre. The family moved to Derby in 1850 and named their new property, "Springfield." They first built a log shanty and then in 1852 a more substantial log house where in 1856 the Kilsyth post office was established with Alexander Fleming the postmaster. He named the community "Kilsyth" after the town which was the final stop on their journey overland in Scotland to the port of Glasgow, on route to the new world.

This frame house was built at "Springfield" in 1864. One of Alexander Fleming's great-grandsons, Stuart Fleming, has had the house moved to his property near Leith along with the chimney and fireplace of the 1852 log house. These artifacts have been faithfully preserved by the family.

The original double hung windows of six-panes-over-six panes, the small transom over the front door, the returned eaves of the roof and the internal chimneys all bespeak "the old country," the classical Renaissance house of western Europe. The house is pristine in its loveliness, a treasure which stands to remind us of one of the outstanding pioneer families of this region.

Photo courtesy Kay Morrison

The Squire House c.1879

Derby Township Pt Lot 8 Con 5

THIS "TUSCAN VILLA" looks eastward from a commanding site in prime farmland. The facade is broken by a two-storey projecting bay topped with a pediment-style roof. The main entrance downstairs is framed by an semicircular fanlight and sidelights. A porch supports a gallery above which is given access by a double door from the upstairs hall. Paired, round-headed windows in the facade are linked by arching stone lintels. Paired brackets support the truncated hip roof which is crowned by a "widow's walk." The superb stonework includes several tall, decorated chimneys.

The land was granted by the Crown in 1847 to a Reverend A. W. H. Rose. James L. Squire from Lowestoft, Suffolk, England acquired the two hundred acre lot for $800 in 1861. His son, Samuel William Squire (1851-1938), who is thought to have built this house, paid $2,000 for the property in 1879. It remained in the Squire family until well into the twentieth century.

THE ANDREW HARDIE HOUSE 1874 (date stone)

Derby Township Pt Lot 7 & Lot 8 Con 4

ANDREW HARDIE, BORN in Sterlingshire, Scotland in 1814, came to Canada in 1832 and to Grey County in 1849. The Derby Township census of 1851 shows that he was settled in a log house on one hundred and fifty acres with his wife Catherine, and their four children. By 1861 they owned two oxen, three cows, two calves and two pigs and were producing grain, maple sugar, butter and pork. By 1874 they had built a commodious brick house and had ten children. Andrew Hardie acted as a Township councillor for seventeen years, was a Liberal by political persuasion and a Presbyterian by religious affiliation.

Such are the bare facts of the life of a man and his family we long to know more about. But perhaps we are safe in assuming that he was brave and adventurous, that he worked hard to fulfill his dream of a better life in a new country, that he was able in his community service and progressive in his views, that he and his wife established a foundation of family upon which future generations would build.

A wide front gable with simple bargeboard and finials is the distinguishing feature of this house. Segmental brick window heads echo the pointed form of the gable. In contrast with these picturesque elements of design, the front entrance has a simple, linear Classical feeling.

THE JOHN DUNCAN HOUSE 1878 (date stone)

Derby Township Pt lot 2 Con 8

THIS LAND WAS granted by the Crown to John Flanagan in 1847. In 1867 it and the adjoining one hundred acres passed into the ownership of John Duncan. It remained in the Duncan family until 1919.

John Duncan was born in Scotland in 1832. By the time of the 1881 Derby Township census, he and his wife Elizabeth had twelve children and had built this vernacular limestone house. The two-sided verandah trimmed with scalloped bargeboard adds lightness and variety to a relatively severe structure. Not only does it improve the appearance of the house but it provides a pleasant place in which to enjoy the outdoor social life of family and friends.

Local history buff, Andrew Armitage, wrote in the Owen Sound Sun Times September 23, 1978 that the Agricultural and Arts Association of Ontario awarded a silver medal to John Duncan in 1889 for his fine farm which, said the judges, was managed with "Scotch shrewdness and industrious habits."

TOWN OF DURHAM

THE GUN HOUSE c.1865

The Town of Durham Plan 502 Lot 24 to 28 Elgin W/S Lot 24 to 27 Albert E/S (283 Durham Rd. E.)

IN 1845 JOHN EDGE purchased the mill site of twenty-two acres on the main Saugeen River east of the Garafraxa Road and another nine hundred and twenty-nine acres in Glenelg Township. Two years later he purchased twenty-one hundred acres in adjoining Bentinck Township. *A History of the Town of Durham, 1842-1994,* compiled by the Durham Historical Committee, relates, page 126, "In a letter to the Colonial Secretary of the Province of Canada, Montreal, dated September 3, 1849, he states that he has spent over two thousand pounds on these properties, including the erection of two mills and other improvements, but has not yet received titles from the land agent for them. His letter was a request that this matter be quickly resolved." He had built his saw mill in 1846 and a flour mill in 1847. In 1856 John Kelly came from Ireland to run the mills.

In the 1860's a lot on the Durham Road East was bought from the Edge Estate by James Gun (born 1834) and his wife, Mary (born 1846). James's parents, Robert Gun and wife, and sisters, Artina and Elizabeth had come to Durham in 1862 from Caithness, Scotland. James Gun was a physician as was his son, Arthur.

James Gun became a beloved figure in the region. He played a major role in the development of the town of Durham, serving on the School Board, setting up a "Model School" in 1877 for teacher training, reorganizing the Mechanic's Institute into the town library (renamed the Durham Public Library in 1895), serving as an Elder in the Presbyterian Church and as the District Health Officer. As early as 1866 Dr. Gun was complaining to the town council that the Saugeen River was being used as a sewer, thereby endangering the health of those who used its waters for drinking and those who swam in it. In 1896 he founded the Durham and District Horticultural Society which functions to this day with a membership of over two hundred.

This house is one of very few in Grey and Bruce Counties of the Neoclassic style. The antique Doric order columns and pilasters of the entrance porch support a classic entablature. Large windows are divided into twenty-four panes. Dentils decorate the cornice under the eaves, and a frieze and corner quoins are executed in raised brickwork. The whole is painted white with contrasting black roof, door, and vestigial shutters — a dramatic presentation of an outstanding heritage house.

283

THE JAMES HUNTER HOUSE "THE HEDGES" C.1867

Town of Durham Con 1 EGR Pt Div. 3 Lot 24 (388 Durham Rd. E.)

THIS HOUSE SERVES as a graphic example of the natural evolution of houses. It began life as a Regency one-storey cottage with a hipped roof. In time the roof was raised and dormers were added to give bedroom space on a second floor. Also a sunroom with a balustraded balcony above was built onto one side of the building. Here is proof that changes can be made to historic houses that very little alter or erode the original character of the house.

The front entrance is in a shallow recess. Fluted pilasters support a broken pediment entablature. A frieze of dentils runs under the eaves, and raised brickwork marks the corners of the house. The interior boasts rooms with generous windows, eleven-and-a-half foot ceilings and massive doors, mouldings and baseboards.

Archibald Hunter (1799-1878), the founder of Durham in 1842, received the Patent from the Crown for fifty acres here in 1851. He had come from Kilbarchan, Renfrewshire, Scotland. In *A History of Grey County,* by E. L. Marsh published in 1931, we are told that Hunter built a log shanty on his land and after one winter returned south leaving this note on his door, "Gone to the United States to bring back my family." He built a stopping place which he named, The British Hotel, on the main corner of Durham in the 1840's. It was a log building of about twenty-four feet by sixty feet. Later he built a stone hotel on the same lot with verandahs on three sides on both first and second levels.

His son, James Hunter (1840-1891), a graduate of Upper Canada College, was a dealer in "staple and fancy dry goods, groceries, hardware, boots and shoes, ploughs and shares," (*A Poetical Directory of Businesses in Mount Forest, Neustadt, Durham, Owen Sound,* A. G. Churchill, 1863) and a Liberal member of the Legislature for South Grey between 1875 and 1883. He built this house for his bride Katie McDonald, the only granddaughter of the great Canadian explorer, Simon Fraser.

One of their children, Colonel Fraser Hunter, had a remarkable military career. So remarkable, in fact, that it is worth repeating verbatim this excerpt from *A History of the Town of Durham, 1842-1994,* published by the Durham Historical Committee (page 101).

"After graduating from Upper Canada College and The Royal Military College, Kingston, Colonel Hunter made his way to England to enlist in the Royal Indian Army. He was required to outfit himself with uniforms and accoutrements at his own expense, and he served as a Bengal Lancer for over thirty years. Colonel Hunter eventually became Deputy Surveyor-General for India. During his military career he saw action on several fronts. In addition to several battles in India, he fought in the Boxer Rebellion in China and was present at the Relief of Peking. In 1914 Fraser Hunter was Squadron Commander in Northwest Frontier operations. He fought with the First and Fourth Armies and joined the Air Force. He spent two years as Chief of Staff to British Forces in Persia. In 1917 he served in Russia and witnessed the start of the Bolshevik Revolution, was present at the evacuation of Petrograd, and helped carry the Czarist ciphers to Washington via Trans-Siberian Railroad and Vladivostok. Colonel Hunter was fluent in Hindustani, Persian, Afghan, Chinese and Japanese; and he had a working knowledge of four other languages. On returning to Canada he became the Liberal Member of the Legislature for St. Patrick's Riding, Toronto. On retiring he returned to The Hedges where he died in 1959."

The Henry Parker House "Idylwilde" c.1875

The Town of Durham Plan 502 Lot 26 to 27 Kincardine W/S Pt lot 26 Pt lot 27 Elgin W/S (385 Durham Rd. E.)

HERE IS A PICTURESQUE, two-storey, ell house set on a large property amongst mature trees. Its High Victorian design vocabulary includes a massive glazed double-door entrance, winged brackets, bargeboard and paired round-headed windows in the gable, two bay windows, and a verandah topped by a balcony given access from the second floor by another glazed double-door. Such a house was built to impress and at the same time to accommodate a large family.

The 1881 Census of the Town of Durham lists Henry Parker, born in 1836, as an immigrant from Bentham, Yorkshire, England along with his wife Elizabeth. He came to Upper Canada in 1857 and became a landowner in Durham. He also acquired a farm in Bentinck Township west of Durham where, in 1881, he helped establish a brickyard under the name, The Samuel Wright Brickyard. Here "yellow" or buff brick was made and supplied to many buildings in Durham, very likely including his own house.

After completing an apprenticeship in the drug business Henry Parker established a branch of the Parker & Cattle Drugstore on Garafraxa Street, Upper Town in Durham in 1860. Other branches in Owen Sound, Goderich and Paris were established by his brothers, S. John Parker and Joseph W. Parker, along with a friend they had met on their passage from England, Mr. George Cattle. The company was reorganized in 1869 under the name, Parker & Co.

The Poetical Dictionary of Businesses in Mount Forest, Neustadt, Durham and Owen Sound, written by A. G. Churchill and published in 1863 in Owen Sound has this to say about this early drug store chain:

"Drugs, medicine line, whiskey, brandy and wine,
Prescriptions for healing disease,
Cuts, fevers and cramps, coal oil and fine lamps,
Lacquers, paints, coffees and teas.

Bar larder for rooms, essential perfumes,
Good books for to read and believe,
All colours and shades of dye stuffs to trade,
And all the materials to weave."

According to *A History of the Town Of Durham, 1842-1994,* Parker was a councillor for the north ward of Durham in the first Town Council in 1872. He helped to found the Durham and District Horticultural Society in 1896 and he played a major role in bringing the Wellington Georgian Bay Railroad from Palmerston to Durham in 1880.

THE ARCHIBALD MACKENZIE HOUSE c.1869

Town of Durham Plan 500 E Pt Lot 13 Countess W/S (312 Lambton St. W.)

GEORGE JACKSON ACQUIRED land here in 1857. He was a celebrated pioneer in Grey County. Born in Hutton, Yorkshire, England in 1809, he came to Canada in 1844 and was appointed Crown Lands Agent for Grey and Bruce Counties in 1848 with his office in the town of Durham. He was the first Reeve of Bentinck Township, an office which he retained for many years. During this period he also served as Warden of Grey County. He then served, with brief interruptions, as the member from Grey County in the Legislative Assembly of the United Canadas from 1854 to 1867 and in the House of Commons from 1867 until shortly before his death in 1885.

In 1868 he sold his property on Lambton Street to Archibald and Sarah Mackenzie. Part of their house served as the Durham Post Office and Mackenzie was postmaster from 1869 until his death in 1899. The house has been occupied by Mackenzie descendants since it was built.

It is a substantial two-storey vernacular Georgian house made of red and buff brick from the Wright brickyards. The house is distinguished by a four-column portico at the front entrance. Fluted columns of the Doric Order stand on double bases and support a moulded entablature roof.

The Cochrane-Jamieson House "Bon Accord" 1867

Town of Durham Plan 500 E Pt Lot 13 Elgin W/S (294 Lambton St. E.)

THIS VERNACULAR GEORGIAN house, with its additional space at the rear for servants' quarters and a medical office, has considerable presence. It is said to have been built in six months by a work force of twenty men. The stone was hauled from an Owen Sound quarry by horse and wagon. The name, "Bon Accord" was given to it in the year it was built as recognition of the Confederation of Canada.

Its owner, Adam Cochrane, came to Canada with his brothers Alexander and Robert from Eagleshome, Renfrewshire, Scotland. Adam and Alexander were co-founders of the Inkerman Foundry and Ironworks in Durham and Alexander became the first mayor in 1872.

In 1885, Adam and Grace Haggert Cochrane sold their property to Dr. David Jamieson (1856-1942), who had come to Durham in 1878. As well as practicing medicine, Dr. Jamieson was the Reeve of Durham (1885-86) and one of the founders of the Durham Furniture Company. He served as the Conservative Party member of the Legislative Assembly for Grey South from 1898 -1919 and 1923-1926, and was Speaker of the House from 1914 to 1919. His Speaker's Chair and Robe are in the collection of the Grey County-Owen Sound Museum. Jamieson also worked for many years as Chairman of the Mothers' Allowance and Old Age Pension Commissions. He acquired some three hundred and fifty acres of land at nearby Wilder's Lake and there he planted two hundred thousand trees. David and Grace Jamieson's son, Bradshaw Jamieson, continued his father's medical practice and residence in the house.

The house displays attributes of the Georgian style, heightened by Gothic Revival and Italianate details which were to become more and more the fashion in this region as the century drew on. It is a two-storey structure with a hipped roof and tall decorative chimneys rising from within each side wall. Wide eaves are supported by brackets and the windows are paired (Italianate). The advancing central bay rises to a gable containing a pointed arch window (Gothic Revival).

Superb stonework distinguishes the house. The facade is composed of cut and coursed limestone and the remaining walls of rubble work. The facade openings are surrounded by smoothly dressed stone slabs and the recessed entrance is flanked by stone Tuscan columns. The same Roman order is continued in the verandah and the upstairs gallery which was added to the house in 1906. The effect of house and verandah combined is one of splendid elegance.

294

THE ARCHIBALD MCLELLAN HOUSE c.1875

Town of Durham Plan 500 Pt Lot 14 Pt Lot 15 Queen W/S (132 Queen St. N.)

THE FRONT ELEVATION of this apparently diminutive Regency cottage is deceiving. Actually, the house stretches out to the rear to provide for ample living space. The front facade, though, is classic in its careful symmetry — a low hipped roof, a generous entrance with transom and sidelights and a columned, sheltering porch. Gothic Revival elements have been added in the form of a gable centred by a quatrefoil attic ventilator. The brickwork at the corners and over the windows has been painted white — a fashion of the 1880's.

Archibald McLellan was the first school teacher at Latona school in the 1850's. He became the Reeve of Durham in 1872 and is described in the 1880 Durham Assessment Roll as a Land Agent.

EGREMONT TOWNSHIP

THE EDWARD HENDERSON HOUSE C.1875

Egremont Township Lot 12 Concession 16

EGREMONT TOWNSHIP IS located on the southern edge of Grey County which, itself, is about one hundred and fifty kilometers from south to north. It is drained by two branches of the Saugeen River and is high in elevation. The result is that this township records the fewest frost-free days of any township in southwestern Ontario — a challenge to its industrious farmers.

Robert Henderson (born 1799) and his wife Robina Murray (born 1810) left Callishield, Scotland in 1830 bound for Halton County in Upper Canada. Several of their children who settled in Egremont Township were among the first wave of settlers who pushed northward in the 1850's and 1860's. Son Edward (1838-1926) and his wife Catherine Rutherford (1844-1912) established themselves on this lot and concession in 1864 and received the Crown Patent in 1870.

The style of the house, and particularly the style of the verandah, point toward a building date of about 1875 in this region. The roughcast exterior covers the original fieldstone construction. Incised markings on the roughcast simulate brick, an interesting exercise in trompe l'oeil. The house is considerably enhanced by the front verandah with its bell-cast roof, original wooden treillage supports and dainty gingerbread brackets.

The William Caulfield House c.1870

Egremont Township Part Lots 17 & 18 Concession 8

THE COUNTY OF GREY DIRECTORY published in Owen Sound by W.W. Smith in 1865 shows one William Caulfield residing on this property. The Patent from the Crown became his in 1867 and the land remained in the family until 1925.

His house is built of delicately coloured fieldstone of various sizes which, nevertheless, are carefully coursed on the front facade. This stonework is enhanced with sawn stone quoins and door and window trim. The sides of the house and the rear summer kitchen exhibit more random stonework. Reserving the most impressive material and workmanship for the front of the house is a practice sometimes still followed today. One shows one's best face to the world.

Generous windows and Gothic Revival bargeboard in the front gable which is centered by a kingpin add interest to this sturdy dwelling-place.

THE GEORGE NEAL HOUSE 1870

Egremont Township Part Lot 8 Concession 1 EGR

THE STORY IS TOLD of how, a few years ago, a workman who was repairing mortar in the stonework of this house, chiseled the date from the datestone as a favour to the startled owner. The workman believed that the older a house the less its resale value; that if it is possible, a new owner should be kept ignorant of the date of the building of the house. In fact, quite the reverse is true if the building has been well maintained. Solid, handmade and beautiful artifacts, such as this house, endure in value.

Its style is enlivened by colour and design detail. The onlooker takes pleasure in the carefully cut fieldstone placed according to colour, in the segmented lintels above the doors and windows, in the graceful Gothic window of the gable, in the moulded frieze and in the transom and sidelights of the front entrance. George Neal built well and for the future.

SPRINGBROOK – THE JAMES MYLES JR. HOUSE 1878 (date stone)

Euphrasia Township Lot 12 Con 5

JAMES SR. AND Elizabeth Myles came to Canada from Ireland in about 1837 with their three children, two born in Ireland and one in the United States. Three more were born in Toronto before they came to Euphrasia Township in about 1845 and by 1851 their family of eight children was complete.

James Myles Jr., their first son and the builder of this house, was born in Ireland in 1830. The deeds to his one hundred and fifty acres are dated 1867 and 1871 and, according to the *Grey County Atlas* of 1880, his assets were valued at the surprisingly high figure of $12,000. He and his wife raised five daughters; Martha, Margaret Ann, Mary, Sarah, and Priscilla.

The outward, lyrical expression of this dry Myles' family geneology is a lovely fieldstone house located in the Beaver Valley close to the village of Kimberly. It is a prototype of its period. Grafted onto a vernacular three-bay Georgian house are Gothic Revival design elements — the awning-roofed verandah, the lacy bargeboard and pointed arched window in the gable, and the asymmetrical mass of the T-shaped structure. Local historians claim that the segmental brick voussoirs over the windows are a sign of the prosperity of the owner because the main building material, fieldstone, was harvested free from the property but brick had to be purchased.

The George Vickers House c.1875

Euphrasia Township Lot 28 Con 3

UNDER THE TREATY of October, 1818, the Ojibway Nation surrendered a tract of land of 1,592,000 acres which later became the Townships of Artemesia, Collingwood, Euphrasia, Osprey, Proton and St. Vincent (the far eastern portion of Grey County). Sixteen thousand acres of that land was secured from the Crown by the Canada Company, of which this two hundred acre parcel was a part.

George Vickers (1819-1905) and his wife, Mary Ann (1824-1869) bought the west half of the lot in 1853 for £200. In 1901 the one hundred acre parcel was passed on to one of their nine children, Albert, and his wife Hannah. Their son Noah inherited the property in 1946. Finally, it passed out of the family when it was sold by Noah Vickers for $10,500 in 1965.

The solid, buff brick house looks westward away from the historic road on which it is located — "The Old Mail Road." It is a handsome two-storey structure with later additions. The generic centre entrance is lit by transom and sidelights. Large windows are slightly arched and finished with segmental voussoirs. The corner quoins are raised.

THE SAMUEL PERRETT HOUSE c.1863

Euphrasia Township Pt Lot 26 Con 2

RICHARD PERRETT (various spellings appear in official documents) was born in 1800 in Ireland and his wife, Jane in 1828. They settled in Euphrasia in the late 1840's having come from Ireland to New Brunswick and then King Township, Upper Canada. Richard Perrett died at the early age of fifty-nine but his son Samuel, one of five children, acquired a Crown Patent to the land in July 1862 and proceeded to build this typical, board and batten house. What is not typical, however, is the lovely Neo-Classic front entrance. Fortunately the glazing of the transom and sidelights was protected for many years by a covering of siding only to be discovered by a new owner in the early 1970's. Pilasters support the entablature. Above the Neo-Classic doorway is a pointed Gothic window in a gable trimmed with Gothic bargeboard and finial. The combination of these Gothic and Classical elements give the facade of this house a unique charm.

The tail of the house has been raised to the full two storeys and a found doorway was added, which closely resembles the front entrance.

The Perrett establishment was a stopping place for travelers because of its location at the conjunction of the second line and The Old Mail Road and because of the availability of water from the spring on the southeast side of this enchanting property.

TOWN OF FLESHERTON

THE JOHN HENRY HEARD HOUSE c.1865

Town of Flesherton Plan 818 Lot 12 (15 Durham Street)

THIS ROUGHCAST GEORGIAN house is dramatic in its classical simplicity. Distinguishing features are a pilastered doorway with transom and sidelights, milled window casings whose tops echo the pediment of the doorway, a gable roof with wide eaves and a pair of internal chimneys at either side of the two-storey rectangular mass of the house.

John Henry Heard (1829-1904) was born in Schapp, Cornwall, England and came to Canada in 1856. He married Catharine White in 1860 and moved to Flesherton where he established Heard's Carriage Works, a major business in the town. After his death, his son, John Alexander, continued the business until 1936. The present owner of the house is John Henry's granddaughter.

THE ARMSTRONG/HICKLING HOUSE c.1890

Town of Flesherton Plan 39 Pt Block E Lot 1,2,3,4 (16 Sydenham Street)

THE QUEEN ANNE REVIVAL STYLE, loosely based on the architecture of the era of Queen Anne, first appeared in this region in the late 1880's. The style remained popular until the beginning of World War I. It is characterized by a picturesque manipulation of forms — towers, bays, intersecting rooflines, multiple dormers, decorated chimney stacks, verandahs and galleries.

This house is a prime example of the style. The square tower which rises two and a half-storeys has a flaring roof which is further ornamented with dormers and supported by flared brackets. One-storey three-sided bay windows advance from front and side elevations while second-floor bays add variety to the roofline. Tall circular chimney stacks have projecting top courses of brick. Also notable is the polychromatic brickwork typical of several Flesherton houses. The patterned red and buff brick is highlighted by linear courses of black brick.

John Armstrong bought this property in 1879. Born in 1831, he had come from Kilkenny County, Ireland to Grey County in 1865. He married Elizabeth Wilson and they had nine children. During his lifetime he worked as a teacher, a Division Court Clerk, a Justice of the Peace and the Treasurer of Artemesia Township.

One of his sons, W. A. Armstrong, was a builder who developed an extensive lumber business. He followed his father as Treasurer of the Township and established a jewelry store in Flesherton.

In 1891 Fred H. W. Hickling came to Flesherton from London, England. He married Adelaide Armstrong and, after her death, her sister Dorothy. He established Hickling's Store in a building erected by W. A. Armstrong in 1911, and remained in business for sixty-three years. He also served as Treasurer of the Town of Flesherton. The property remains in the family.

Photo by Ruth Cathcart

GLENELG TOWNSHIP

THE JOHN B. MORDAN/WILLIAM VESSIE HOUSE c.1855

Glenelg Township Lot 18 Div 3 Con 1 EGR

GLENELG TOWNSHIP'S FIRST registered settler, Edward Boulton, came here in 1841 and obtained the Patent for his land from the Crown in 1847. In order for him to receive his free grant to this fifty acres, he was required to occupy the property, to clear at least one third of it, and to plant at least one crop — all in the time span of four years. Obviously the rules were bent a little in his case because it was six years between the date of his location ticket and the date of his deed. Settlers were also allowed to reserve for purchase the adjacent fifty acres to their granted land.

John B. Mordan bought the property in 1849 for £100 and built his house not many years later. Between 1901 and 1978 it was the property of the William Vessie family.

It is a typical Regency Cottage, beautiful in its proportions, low in mass, and symmetrical in design. The building material is stone which is pleasingly subtle in colour. Such a house was built not just to give shelter but to give pleasure to its inhabitants and to passersby for generations to come.

The John Fallaise House c.1865

Glenelg Township West Pt lot 11 Con 5 NDR

LAND REGISTRY RECORDS show that this Crown land of one hundred acres was acquired by Henry Lutz in 1862, although it was probably settled some years before that. He immediately sold off the east and west halves for $250 each. John and Elizabeth Fallaise bought the west half and here they built their house and raised their six children. The property remained in the family until 1926.

The house is a sturdy example of what is sometimes referred to as "Wilderness Georgian" and is built of mellow stone. The front door is flanked by transom and sidelights in order to light the centre hall. Windows are placed to light the symmetrical interior layout. Although the house appears from the road to be modest in size it is actually built on a slope which provides for an extra storey in the rear. At one time a pretty verandah with an awning roof and treillage supports added interest to the front elevation.

The William Ritchie House c.1868

Glenelg Township Pt Lot 36 Con 2 EGR

ALTHOUGH THE PATENT for the east half of this farm was granted by the Crown in 1856 and the Patent for the adjacent fifty acres was granted in 1868, William Ritchie and his wife, Margaret Kelly, actually settled here in 1848. They had come from County Tyrone in Ireland.

When their log cabin burned in 1868 the family immediately set to work to build this fine two-storey stone house with its one-storey stone tail. Examples of this house design can be found all over Grey County. The style has been aptly named, "Wilderness Georgian."

The Ritchie parents with their nine children played an active role in the community. According to *A History of Glenelg Township,* page 187, son George was a popular fiddler and at one time the president of the local Agricultural Society. A daughter Jane was a well-known practical nurse who attended to the needs of the sick in her community.

Photo courtesy of *A History of Glenelg Township,* 1985

GEORGE RITCHIE WITH HIS FIDDLE

THE DANIEL KNECHTEL HOUSE c.1910

Hanover Lot 12 Pt Lot 11 Plan 701 (553 10th Ave.)

DANIEL KNECHTEL CAME from Waterloo County to Hanover in 1864 and two years later initiated what was to become one of the largest manufacturing companies in Canada, The Knechtel Furniture Company. He and his sons were admirable town boosters. They gave land for the sites of the Hanover Library and the Hanover Memorial Hospital. They also donated land on the corner of Mary and Durham Streets for the English Baptist Church. Daniel Knechtel served as the town's first Reeve in 1900 and later (1909-1911) became the mayor.

Daniel and his brother Joshua started a cement plant using marl, soil consisting of clay and carbonate of lime from the nearby Marl Lakes. The marl was also used as a polish for cutlery and glass. Clarence Ellis in *Hanover Remembers — Sketches of the Past,* relates the amusing story of a couple of industrious gentlemen who came through the area by horse and buggy carrying a quantity of bags. "They filled them with dry marl and the following summer they returned to the neighbourhood selling silver polish and window cleaner to the very farmers who owned the marl in the first place!"

This modest cottage, built of cement blocks, was the last home of Daniel Knechtel. Its distinguishing feature is the curved portico effect of the front porch and above it, the echoing curved dormer.

553

THE SAMUEL FELLMAN HOUSE c.1886

Hanover Lot 5 Plan 701 (503 10th Ave.)

THIS YELLOW BRICK HOUSE, built by Samuel Fellman who is listed in the 1880 *Atlas of Grey and Bruce Counties,* page 81, as a painter, would be unremarkable if it were not for its corner front entrance above which is a second-storey pointed door necessitating a third gable.

The well-known Canadian artist, Carl Fellman Schaefer, grew up in this house. Schaefer, born in Hanover in 1903, studied at the Ontario Collage of Art under Arthur Lismer, J.E. H. MacDonald, George Reid and J. W. Beatty. When he graduated in 1924 he celebrated with a small show of oil sketches in the firehall at Hanover. In *A Concise History of Canadian Painting,* Dennis Reid writes, page 178, "By the Depression Schaefer was raising a family and able to find employment only as a part-time teacher, and so to save money, every summer and winter holiday break from 1932 through 1939 he and his family lived with his grandparents back in Hanover. It was a period of reaffirmation of traditional values and of assertive creativity, resulting in a long series of stunning canvases." One of his best-known paintings of this period is "Ontario Farmhouse" which is in the collection of the National Gallery. His experience as a war artist attached to the RCAF during World War II when he had flown on night bombing raids, had a profound effect upon his art, according to Dennis Reid. "His work remained dark … and kept to themes of violence."

THE JOHN MCINNIS HOUSE c.1900

Holland Township Lot 1 Con 1 WTSR

IN ABOUT 1850, JOHN MCINNES married Margaret Miller in Glasgow, Scotland and they emigrated to Canada. He had been trained as a cobbler in the old country and continued that trade in the new land, adding the skills of blacksmithing and farming because shoes were not a priority for the earliest settlers. As the township history *The Paths That Led To Holland Township*, page 45, explains — "Shoes were considered a luxury and the pioneers would go barefoot until they came to a village when they would put on their shoes."

McInnes secured his land by Crown deed in 1856. A log house was built and later, in 1864, a fine barn. The house with its great open fireplace became the meeting place in the community. Friends and strangers alike were fed and warmed here. Presbyterian prayer meetings and the first township council met in the commodious kitchen.

Six generations of McInnises have occupied this land. George McInnis Jr. built the present house which is sheathed with pine cove siding. The parlour floor is made of one and a half inch pine boards secured with square oak pegs driven into round holes. The present drive shed was formerly a smithy and wagonwright shop.

The Michael McCann House c.1860

Holland Township Lot 66 Con 2 WTSR

About 1855, Michael McCann (1807-1892) with his wife Mary Patterson and their children Kate, Mary, John and Tom came from Donegal, Ireland to settle in Holland Township. They received a free grant of fifty acres and bought the fifty acres across the road. The government was opening townships along the path of the newly surveyed Toronto-Sydenham Road, roughly Shelburne to Chatsworth, by making free grants of land accompanied by certain settlement duties. Most of the old Toronto-Sydenham Road is now in use as Highway 10.

The story of the construction of the old settlement roads in this region is illuminating. As each road was surveyed, the trees were cut and laid across the trail in corduroy fashion, with earth and stones piled on top. The township history, *The Paths That Led To Holland Township,* page 7, reads: "In some portions, travelers had to find their way by means of marks blazed on the trees and over swamps not yet bridged, by a layer of logs. Even in the cleared roads, tree stumps still protruded until they could be removed and rolled to one side."

The McCann's first shelter would likely have been a log shanty, perhaps without windows. This more permanent log house was built around 1860. It not only had generous windows, but it had a second floor for bedrooms and a first floor kitchen/woodshed built onto one side. It was occupied continuously by McCann's descendants through Michael's and Mary's son John, until 1962.

The Thomas Mitchell House c.1890

Holland Township Village of Berkeley (Pt Lot 60 Con 1 SWTSR)

THOMAS MITCHELL, WHO at one time owned mills in Liverpool England and in Holland Centre, Corbetton, and Parry Sound in Canada, purchased the Berkeley Mill in March 6, 1889. His house was built at about the same time.

It presents a pristine appearance to the community. Its wood siding is painted white, the vestigial Gothic decoration is highlighted in a mid-green, the roof is black. Thus this large ell-shaped house with its two front entrances, its gables, verandah and bay window is unified by the simple use of colour.

The Marshall House c.1880

Holland Township Pt Lot 1 Pt Lot 2 Con 12 (Village of Walters Falls)

Part of the appeal of this house lies in its weathered shingle cladding. However, the shingles are but the third layer covering its bones. The bones are the stud walls which were infilled with a mixture of mortar and gravel. The French termed such infilling, "colombage." The English called it "half-timbering." The term used by local inhabitants in Grey County is "grouting." The walls were then sheathed with two layers of vertical planks — the outer layer of boards were battened. A twentieth century owner "modernized" the exterior with a layer of insulbrick. That fake brick cladding was later covered with cedar shingles. A benefit of these layers of cladding is improved insulation.

John Walter arrived in the area, now centered by the village of Walters Falls, in 1852 where he took up almost three hundred acres from the Crown. The Patent was registered in September 1860. His land was located around the south branch of the Bighead River. Soon several mills were put into operation. The village itself is a place of considerable charm because of its river valley location and because of its relative isolation from urban centres in the County.

The Township history, *The Paths That Led To Holland Township,* volume 1 (page 192) tells this story: "John Walter was a gardener for a family in England by the name of Payne. Young John fell in love with his employer's daughter, Elizabeth. The Payne family tried to discourage the love affair but a union was made and John and Elizabeth left their home in England and came to Canada." Here is a tale of love, courage and initiative; a tale which was repeated time and again in our settlement area. The status ridden society of the old world was the deciding factor in the decision made by many to emigrate to the new world and, just as in the case of the migration of Vietnam war resisters to Canada in this century, our country has benefitted by their settling here.

KEPPEL TOWNSHIP

THE JOHN ELLIOTT HOUSE c.1895

Keppel Township Lot 3 Con 15

THIS TWO-STOREY, quarried stone house is a fine example of its type — a multi-gabled, ell shaped structure built of a warm-hued limestone with carefully colour-matched mortar. At one time, as the drawing by esteemed local artist Douglas Wood shows, a front verandah was tucked into the ell, providing shelter for the front door and breaking the height of the building. Bargeboard once enlivened the eaves of the gables. Without these accoutrements the house appears rather too severe.

John Elliott and his wife, Eliza Ann Alexander, raised six children here. He served on the Keppel Township Council for many years and was Reeve from 1900 to 1903.

Drawing by Douglas Wood, 1968

THE MILLS/HEWITSON HOUSE 1894 (date stone)

Keppel Township Lot 13 Con B

THIS HOUSE IS DISTINGUISHED by its accomplished brickwork — comparable to that of the great Edwardian houses of Toronto, particularly in the Annex district. Here the mason has used a "common bond" — that is, five rows of the long or "stretcher" side of the brick then a row of bricks on end or "headers." Decorative brickwork highlights the centre round headed window and the angles of the bays on the second floor. All of the windows have stone sills and segmental brick voussoirs.

The Crown Patent for this one hundred acre property was granted to Francis Mills in October, 1876 when he was 48 years old. It remained in the family until 1918 when John Hewitson bought it for $7,500.

In 1892 the township assessment roll noted that seventy-five of Francis Mills' one hundred acres were cleared, that he had a two acre orchard and twenty acres planted in fall wheat. The house is a reflection of his prosperity.

The Case/Loughleen House c.1890

Kepple Township Pt Lot 5 on Plan 16R 4572 Concession 15

THE STORY OF THIS house attests to the solidity of its quarried stone structure. It was completely gutted by fire in 1966 and remained a stone shell open to the weather until 1992 when the house was rebuilt within the walls. One is grateful to the present owners who recognized an opportunity to bring the house back to life and acted on it.

The design could not be more simple — a cube with a hipped roof. The masonry consists of dressed, uniform stones laid in coursed ranges. Segmental stone voussoirs give the structure a wide-awake look.

Joseph Case received one hundred and twenty-one acres from the Crown by Patent in April, 1878. Two years later he divided his land between his sons Andrew and Joseph. Three years after that, Andrew sold his share to his brother for $100 and in 1889 Joseph Case Jr. and his wife mortgaged their land for $1000 in order to build their "four-square" house.

In 1920, John A. Loughleen bought the property for $6,000. His parents, Robert and Elza Jane McIlveen, had come to the New World from near Lake Loughleen in Killarney, Ireland. John, fourth of five children, made this family home the social centre of the community. His daughter, Bernice, has written for the Clavering Tweedsmuir History: "A few enjoyable things I remember were the dances and showers held at our home and the good square dances called by my brother Chud. My uncles Frank Loughleen and John Lisk were pretty good on the fiddles. The old stone house burned in 1966 — pictures and treasures were all lost, we all felt bad about that, but all have wonderful memories about our home in Clavering."

THE JOSEPH DAVIDSON HOUSE C.1906

Keppel Township Pt Lot 26 Con 24 Hamlet of Lake Charles

JOSEPH DAVIDSON (1812-1903) and his wife, Mary Campbell (1808-1902) came from Dunfermline, Scotland to Canada in 1845. They settled first at Bowmanville, then at Mitchell and then Listowel before retiring to Oxendon, Kepple Township. Joseph Jr. born in 1850, the oldest of their children, purchased this property in 1887 for $3,600. The house was built after he and his wife made a visit to Scotland. Norval Davidson, a grandson, is quoted as saying *Owen Sound Sun Times,* August 31, 1973: "An uncle of mine drew up the plans and three uncles and my father, as well as some people around here, pitched in and helped build it. Materials were found on the farm for the two-and-a-half storey, fourteen room house. The floors and paneling are made from ash trees and the outside cement blocks were made right on the site. I don't really know what prompted my grandfather to build a copy of a castle. I guess he was tired of living in log houses."

Today, the house is occupied by Joseph Davidson's great granddaughter and her family. It is remarkable chiefly for its crenellated tower — no doubt a reminder to the family of "dear old Scotland."

THE JAMES SIMS HOUSE 1904 (date stone)

Keppel Township Lot 13 Con 18

JAMES SIMS (1841-1935) had this substantial stone house built when he was sixty-three years old. He and his wife, Eliza Atkey (1863-1913) and their four children came to the property in 1885 from a concession several miles north.

Scottish stonemasons built him a two-storey, ell-shaped house with the date-stone prominently set between two upstairs windows. The interior layout reflects a mixture of lifestyles from the old and new lands. The large, tongue-and-groove wood lined kitchen dominated by a wood-fired cooking range is typical of Ontario farmhouses. However, the front and back staircases harken back to the old country where servants were expected to use the narrow, steep back stairs while the more generously designed front stairs were reserved for members of the family.

Houses built between about 1895 and 1925 in this region boast of the first "picture windows" — often topped by a stained glass panel. The clear glass in this picture window is wavy and pitted, indicating that sheet glass makers had not yet perfected the manufacture of larger windows.

North Keppel Heights – The Daniel Davidson House

1902 (date stone)

Keppel Township   Pt Lot 40 Con 24

The Crown Patent for this property was issued in 1888 to Daniel Davidson, brother of Joseph, the builder of the "castle" at Lake Charles. Their parents were Scots who came to Canada in 1845. According to Land Registry records, Daniel Davidson occupied this property from the year 1875 and took out several mortgages on it before securing the Patent.

The house is built of quarried stone found, no doubt, nearby. There is no shortage of such building material in this township which has been dubbed "Stoney Keppel."

Multiple frame additions have been appended to the original stone structure which, in itself, was a substantial two-storey house with a hipped roof capped by a balustraded gallery. The ensemble is a sympathetic amalgam of the old and the new. This is an imposing house complemented by a superb barn set in an extensive garden graced by mature trees.

The Dawe House c.1890

Keppel Township Lot 14 Con 18

THE CROWN DEED TO this seventy-nine acre property was issued to Joseph Kerr in 1876 for the sum of $133.00. After passing through several hands it was bought by James A. Dawe in 1884.

Dawe was born in Hastings County of English parents in 1856. He married Mary Elizabeth Cronkite of Belleville in 1883 and they came directly to Keppel Township. His obituary writer described James Dawe as a Conservative, a Methodist and a staunch Orangeman. "During his fifty years residence in Keppel Township he seldom, if ever, missed a 12th of July parade."

Their son, Herbert (1890-1967) took over the farm in 1919. He had married Harriet Tambling in 1910 and was known in the community as an ardent hunter and fisherman. The farm remained in the Dawe name until 1994 — one hundred and ten years.

The ell-shaped house is situated at the end of a long lane. Its rosy-red brick is set off by buff brick at the corners and over the window and door openings. It is well lit by many large windows and embellished by two pretty verandahs. The arable land behind the south-facing house borders on shallow, reedy Mountain Lake — surely one of the most amusingly misnamed geographical sites in this area where the topography is absolutely flat.

TOWN OF MARKDALE

KNARSBORO HALL c.1880

Markdale Plan 582 Block C Pt Lot 29 (63 Main St. E.)

THIS IMPRESSIVE FRENCH Second Empire house displays the full design vocabulary of that style. Its third storey concave mansard roof is punctuated by dormer windows and its tower is capped by a convex mansard roof. Decorative brickwork adds interest to the facades and chimneys. There are twenty-two round headed windows with each carved keystone representing a different flower. Side porches are fully articulated. The house is an expression of the increasing wealth and sophistication of its owner more than simply a commodious dwelling place. Dr. Thomas Simpson Sproule (1843-1917) engaged the Toronto architect, Marshal B. Aylesworth, to design Knarsboro Hall which he wish to be modeled after a Scottish mansion of the same name.

Markdale Ont. The Crossroads of Grey, published in 1988, tells the story of the man and his house (pages 157-59). We are told that Sproule was born in King Township, Upper Canada in 1843. His father, James Sproule, had come from County Tyrone in Ireland in 1836. Son Thomas graduated from the University of Michigan at Ann Arbour and studied medicine at Victoria College in Coburg, Ontario. He graduated in 1868 and came to Markdale in 1869.

His career was full and diverse. As well as practicing medicine he entered the retail drug business, flour and saw milling, farming and stock raising. He served on the Town Council and was elected the Member of Parliament for Grey East between 1878 and 1915. His political career was capped by his service as Speaker of the House of Commons from 1911 until his retirement in 1915. He had served under seven Prime Ministers.

He is described in the town history as being a Methodist, a Conservative, and a zealous Orangeman. In fact, he was Sovereign Grand Master in British North America for ten years and World President of the Orange Council for three years.

Sproule's wife was Mary Alice Flesher, daughter of W.K. Flesher, Member of Parliament for Flesherton from 1872 until 1880. They had one daughter, Lillie.

THE HILL HOUSE c.1896

Markdale Plan 582 Block Lot 6 & 7 (66 Toronto St. S.)

ACCORDING TO *Markdale Ont. The Crossroads of Grey* (page 169), Solomon Hill (1844-1914) was born in Devonshire, England. He came to Canada with his parents when he was five years old. His father died a week after they landed. His mother remarried and the family moved to the Markdale area in 1855. Solomon Hill was a merchant in Markdale for forty-seven years. He married Sarah Ellen Smith of Trenton and they had four sons and four daughters. He is described in the town history as being a Liberal and an Anglican. In 1894 his son, Frank, entered the family business and expanded it until there were branches in Tara, Alliston, Orangeville, Highgate, Brampton, Stayner, Meaford, Chesley and Eugenia. He also operated seed houses throughout the countryside and became the owner of the Markdale Garage.

At the age of fifty-two Solomon Hill built one of the finest Queen Anne Revival style houses in small-town Ontario. It commands a large corner lot on the main north-south street of the town (Highway 10) and is contained within stone walls topped by an impressive wrought iron fence. Most of the attributes of the Queen Anne Revival Style are here: corner tower with a six-sided roof, multiple gables and dormers, rusticated stonework, advancing and retreating wall planes, porches and balconies, and tall and elaborate chimneys.

THE MARK ARMSTRONG JR. HOUSE c.1892

Markdale Part Lot 101 Con 1 SWTSR (150 Mark St.)

BRICK FOR THIS AND many other Markdale houses was made in Cheeseville at the Bowler Brickyard. Their bricks were identified by the letter "C W B". This house is situated on a one acre property graced by mature trees, especially Norway Spruce. It is a handsome structure with shifting wall planes, gables, paired windows, and a parlour "picture" window surmounted by a stained glass panel. In the *Markdale Standard,* 1894, we read, "The woodwork of the first flat is red oak, oil finish; the kitchen is ash and the second flat is pine, oak grained." Extensive first and second storey porches were built in about 1912 to replace the original entranceway and highly decorative second storey balconet.

Markdale Ont. The Crossroads of Grey, page 6, relates that William Armstrong was born in 1829 in County Monaghan, Ireland and came to Canada with his elder brother and sister-in-law, Mark and Elizabeth (Strain) Armstrong, when he was nineteen years old. He married Margaret Strain in York (Toronto) and came to the Markdale area to take up land adjacent to his brother, Mark, after whom Markdale is named. William and Margaret had eleven children. Their oldest son Mark Jr. built this house on land given to him by his uncle. Alexander Acheson bought the house in 1934 and it remains in the family through his daughter, Lois Henry.

Mark Armstrong Jr. and his brothers established the Armstrong Sawmill and several factories for the manufacture of veneer and crates. In 1906 they provided quarter cut oak flooring for Buckingham Palace. Their six mill buildings were connected by steam pipes and a system of tramways. All was lost in an 1894 fire. The brothers rebuilt — this time with an iron roof, and in 1898 they built another mill east of Flesherton at Rock Mills.

One of the brothers, George Whitfield Armstrong, moved west in 1904 and acquired a tract of twelve thousand acres, one hundred miles north west of Regina. This community became known as "Strongfield," a combination of his names. He invited farmers in Grey county to join him there and many from Markdale, Meaford, Walter's Falls and Feversham did just that.

Vintage photo courtesy of *Markdale Ont. Crossroads of Grey*

The Frederick York House c.1871

Meaford 186 Bayfield (Plan 309 Pt Lot 1554 carried from Lot 2 Plan 74)

THIS SUBSTANTIAL AND colourful fieldstone house has all the attributes one looks for in a Wilderness Georgian style house — symmetry, solidity and simplicity. There are three bays with a central entrance, a shallow pitched and hipped roof, and segmental stone arches over the windows.

Land Registry records show that the property first came into the ownership of William Stephenson and his wife in 1848. Frederick York bought the property in 1871 for $750.00 and took out a mortgage on that date with which to built his fine, stone house. He was the son of Henry York, from Northhampshire, England who had come with his wife and five children to Canada in 1841 — first to Quebec, then to Prince Edward County and finally to settle for good in St. Vincent Township in 1845. One of Frederick York's brothers, William, is known as the author of the book, *Porcupine Trails,* published by The Musson Book Co., Toronto.

A new owner in the early 1900's was Newton Cooper, the mayor of Meaford. In 1924 the Harvey W. McKay family moved into the house. They owned several farms in St. Vincent Township. A daughter, Mrs. Jean Ellis, tells of heating the house with a wood and coal furnace, the kitchen cookstove and the dining room fireplace. It was still uncomfortably chilly in the wintertime. In summer, though, it was comfortably cool. The delicacy of the two tamarack trees planted in front of the house by the McKays soften its stern outline.

THE CLELAND/CLARKE HOUSE c.1880

Meaford 55 Trowbridge Street West (Plan 309 Pt Lot 1051 carried from S of Trowbridge)

DURING THE 1870'S AND 1880'S the Second Empire style became the height of fashion in urban domestic architecture for relatively wealthy Canadians. The name derives from the Second Empire of Napoleon III of France. There, the basic building unit was the apartment house and when the streets of Paris were lined with Second Empire apartment houses a citywide visual unity was achieved.

In 1868 the first official residence of the Lieutenant Governor of Ontario in Toronto was designed in the Second Empire style thus setting the fashion throughout the province. Also American pattern books and Canadian publications helped to establish a taste for this style. "The intangible qualities embodied by these large structures such as stability, wealth, progress, power, and so forth, were desirable associations for aspiring gentlemen." *Second Empire Style in Canadian Architecture* by Christina Cameron and Janet Wright. Parks Canada. Historic Sites: Occasional Papers in Archaeology & History #24.

This example in Meaford is truly outstanding. It retains most of its original attributes. The porch has been altered and one of the double windows in the front has been reduced to a single window. Otherwise it stands in all its original elaborate, high-style dignity. Its asymmetric facade is anchored by two towers capped by shallow hipped roofs and carried upward from main floor bay windows. These main floor windows are surrounded by decorative frames. The second floor boasts ornate dormer windows. Indeed, all the decorative work of the exterior is strongly reminiscent of the American "stick" style in which corners of buildings and windows are emphasized by the application of shaped lumber and painted in contrasting colour. Which brings us to the colour scheme of this fantasy. The rich cream, brown and green combination along with its unique style set it entirely apart from its neighbours. It remains the jewel in the crown of the historic houses of Meaford.

The house was built in the late 1870's by James Cleland who bought the half acre of land for $800. He had served on the St. Vincent Township council, had been Reeve of Meaford from 1872 to 1880, and Mayor from 1886 to 1889. He became the Liberal Member of the Provincial Parliament for North Grey, 1890 to 1894. His wealth was generated from the Cleland Hardware of Meaford and the first private telephone line which he established in Meaford in 1884. Born June 10, 1839 in Glasgow, he came to Meaford in 1857. He married

Sarah Butchart (1840 - 1926) in 1862 and they had six sons; Hugh Robert (hardware merchant), James (Meaford Wheelbarrow Co.), Andrew (died in his early 20's), Frederick A. (Toronto surgeon), Edward (manager of Meaford Steel Products) and Donald (Bank of Montreal).

In September, 1889, Cleland sold to Dr. John G. Clarke who had begun his medical practice in Meaford in 1881, continuing it for nearly fifty years. Dr. Clarke played an active role in the community, serving as its first Medical Officer of Health beginning in the mid-1890's and mayor from 1910 to 1913. He died in October, 1930 leaving his daughter Bertha to continue the family tradition in this wonderful house.

Vintage photo courtesy of *A Pictorial History of the Town of Meaford, 1818-1991*

The Pollard House c.1867

Meaford 91 Denmark Street (Plan 309 N Pt Lot 1187 carried from Lot 5 Collins Street)

THIS IS THE KIND of house a man of parts would build at the time of the establishment of the towns and cities of the Grey and Bruce region. It is a solid, respectable, well-ordered red brick house of two storeys, beautifully lit by large windows and by transom and sidelights at the entrance. When almost all of the countryside was a wilderness an English gentleman, Colonel William D. Pollard, did his part to tame it by imposing this confident structure as his mark on the land.

Tall, shaped chimneys rise from either side of the hipped roof with its narrow eaves. The stone quoining, the cornice and window lintels are all prominent. The handsome porch is a later addition.

Pollard was born in Manchester, England in 1827. He was a public schoolboy who went on to become a solicitor in Masters in Chancery, London. In about 1855 he came to Collingwood where he was manager for three years of the Shale Oil Works and was partner in law with a Mr. Haberly. He arrived in Meaford in 1862 and became its first mayor in 1875 to 1877. He was a staunch Conservative and a militia volunteer achieving the rank of major during the Fenian Raids and thereafter lieutenant-colonel.

Colonel Pollard married three times. His first wife, Mary Smith bore him three children. Jane Taylor, his second wife died in childbirth. He must have built this fine house for his third wife, Rose Fuller, whom he married in 1866. They had six children.

c.1875

Meaford 60 Boucher Street East (Plan 309 Lot 1315 lot 1319 continued from the Mill Reserve)

THE LAND ON WHICH this house was built was known at one time as "Purdy Town" after one Jesse Purdy who, in 1850, acquired from the Crown most of the Government Mill Reserve along the Bighead River in Meaford. He built several mills there including the original woolen mill. He laid out some of his land into a village site, built a road through it and a bridge to cross the river to connect with the town along the line of Sykes Street and became prominent in the affairs of the Meaford. He also built a school in which one of his daughters, Harriet Ann, became the first teacher. His pioneering spirit then drew him farther west — to North Dakota, in fact, where he lived to the great age of ninety-three. His life neatly spanned the nineteenth century as he was born in 1806 and died in 1899.

It is not known who built this house but it is, along with the Bishop house in Owen Sound (see page 146) an utterly charming example of Ontario Gothic Revival. Its steeply pitched roof, gables, bargeboard and decorative brickwork are of the highest order. The structure sits snugly on its site and is surrounded by magnificent mature trees.

The Francis Eberhart House c.1900

Meaford 86 Trowbridge Street West (Plan 309 Lot 960 carried from Lot 13 North of Trowbridge)

THE LAND ON WHICH this house was built was granted by the Crown in 1853 to John Maughan a bigwig in Owen Sound. He sold it very soon after to another influential Owen Sounder, George Snider, for £36. It is thought the house was built by either the Finleys or the Littles, successive owners, before the property was acquired in 1920 by Francis Louis Eberhart, the much loved and esteemed physician who served Meaford for over fifty years.

Born in Seaforth, he came to practice medicine in Meaford in 1916 when he was rejected on health grounds for service in World War I. And here he remained, active in community affairs until his death in 1970.

"The doctor's house" epitomized his status in town. It is a rambling, picturesque, brick edifice of some character. Count the rooflines, the bays, the chimneys. Admire the cornice and winged brackets, the brickwork, the "parade" balcony above the curved porch. (The porch itself is a later addition.) This is Ontario in all its rock-ribbed stability and prosperity.

Dr. Eberhart's office was reached from a separate door off the porch. The main entrance has glazed double doors which lead to a small foyer with a tightly-curved staircase rising to the second floor. Upstairs are four large bedrooms and a bathroom with doorways surmounted by glass transoms. The woodwork is typical for the time. So-called bullseyes mark the upper corners of all the openings. The doors are five-paneled. There is a front and a back staircase.

96

c.1880

Meaford 35 Victoria Crescent (Plan 309 Pt lot 482 Pt Lot 483 carried from Lot 24 Plan 82)

LAND REGISTRY RECORDS show that this property passed from the Crown by Patent in 1850 to brothers Jesse and Hazzard Purdy. Both men became prominent in the community. (Jesse's career is described on page 128.)

The house is said to have sheltered fabled "Beautiful Joe," the dog whose sad life was immortalized by Margaret Marshall Saunders in her famous book of the same name. Saunders was a well-known writer who spent summer vacations in Meaford with relatives. She entered a book contest sponsored by the American Humane Society and won an award of two hundred dollars for BEAUTIFUL JOE. To celebrate the one hundredth anniversary of the publication of the immensely popular book, The Ginger Press of Owen Sound republished it in 1994.

"Beautiful Joe" lies buried close to the Bighead River in the North Grey Conservation Authority park next to this modest house. His grave is marked by a cairn on which is mounted an Ontario historic plaque honouring Margaret Saunders, writer of children's stories about animals and birds, who reminded us of our responsibility to always treat such creatures humanely.

NORMANBY TOWNSHIP

The Robert Rutherford House c.1870

Normanby Township Part lots 22 & 23 Con 5

THE 1871 CENSUS OF Normanby Township shows that Robert Rutherford, born in Scotland in 1833, his wife, Agnes and their two daughters, Hanna and Christina, occupied this one hundred acre lot. They had come here some time in the six previous years because the *1865 Grey Directory* published by W. W. Smith lists the lot as unoccupied up to that time.

A census-taker reports only the facts, of course. And the facts recorded in 1871 were that the Rutherfords produced hay, grains, apples, potatoes and peas, maple sugar, butter, wool, beef, mutton and pork in the previous year. In the few years they had occupied the land they had cleared half of it, built a stone house and a large barn. All of this represents a prodigious amount of labour. It also represents a faith in the land and in their own ability to support themselves. They had what it took to meet the challenges of the pioneer way of life.

Their house has been carefully tended and expanded by the present owner. It serves as another example of the best of our early houses which have been rehabilitated and saved for future generations.

The Leibold House c.1878

Normanby Township Lot 26 Con 6

MORE THAN HALF of the original settlers in Normanby Township came directly from Germany or from Germany via Waterloo County. Martin Leibold and his wife, Justina Barbara, migrated to Preston in Upper Canada from Bavaria in 1851 — seeking respite from the Prussian Wars. Ten years later they found their homestead in Normanby. They knew, along with their fellow German settlers, where to find the best land. We are told in *Normanby Reflections — A History of Normanby Township* pp.100-101, that the Germans settled where the fine hardwoods grew because those trees were supported by the richest soil. We are also told that instead of planting grain amongst the stumps after clearing the land as the British immigrants did, the Germans preferred to completely clear their fields, retaining bordering trees and woodlots for both practical and aesthetic reasons.

The Martin Leibolds received their one hundred acres from the Crown in 1866. It has descended through their son, grandson to the great grandson who is the present owner.

The house, built in about 1878, is one of the strongest examples of a five-bay Georgian-style farmhouses in the region. The recessed front entrance is particularly fine with the original glazing in transom and sidelights. Windows also retain their original glazing. The fieldstones of the front facade, from the window tops to the roofline, are huge. The original stone summer kitchen at the rear has been covered with roughcast and topped with a later brick second-storey.

THE GEORGE GREIN HOUSE 1878 (name and date stone)

Normanby Township Lots 9 & 10 Con 9

GEORGE GREIN WAS born in 1833, the son of Heinrich Grein and Katharina Peters, who came to Canada from Alsfeldt Hassen Dormstadt, Germany in about 1852. George acquired this land from the Crown in 1867 and it stayed within the family until 1945. Known to have been a stonemason as well as a farmer, Grein built his own house and inserted a stone high in a side wall which is incised, G GREIN 1878.

1871 assessment records show that George and Jenny Grein had five children, one hundred and fifty acres of land, of which ninety-five were clear, and a sizable production of grain, hay, peas and potatoes, apples and maple sugar.

Here is another handsome five-bay Normanby Township fieldstone house with a recessed entrance lit by the original glazing of transom and sidelights. Provision was made during the building of the house for a front verandah (a wooden bar was inserted in the stonework to which the verandah roof could be attached). Such a verandah, as well as serving the useful purpose of providing sheltered outdoor living space, also served to cut the height of the building.

The Rueber House c.1885

Normanby Township Lot 5 Con 6

THE FIRST KNOWN settler on this land was a John Nispel who is listed in the *W.W. Smith Directory of Grey County of 1865* as born in 1834, married to Katharina and the father of five children. He sold the property in 1879 to Peter Rueber for the sum of $5,600. The Rueber family retained the farm until 1950.

Their buff brick house is a cubical two-storey structure with a low hipped roof and an extensive two-storey rear appendage. The front entrance is the most pleasing characteristic of the house. Unassuming glazed double doors are surmounted by a glazed transom. This doorway and the porches serve to relieve the plainness of a substantial brick farmhouse.

OSPREY TOWNSHIP

THE THOMAS MCGIRR HOUSE "WILDBERRY FARM" C.1890

Osprey Township Lot 17 Con 14

OSPREY TOWNSHIP IS located on a plateau twelve hundred feet high in the Blue Mountains. Three rivers have their headwaters here — the Saugeen, the Beaver and the Mad. Much of the township is not ideal for farming and that is why, in the days of its settlement, Crown land was sold for as little as $1 an acre with twenty years to pay.

James McGirr acquired the Patent to 114 acres here in 1872. The land remained in the McGirr family until it was sold to John and Thomas Cooper in 1911 for $4200.

Unusual for this tee-shaped house is the extended foyer at the front entrance. It is surmounted by a second-floor balcony which is sheltered by an overhanging gable. Contrasting colour brickwork defines the windows and gives interest to the exterior elevations. The encompassing verandah is a recent addition.

"Hillside House" c.1900

Osprey Township Plan 231 Lot 17 W of Mill Village of Feversham

Feversham, originally named "Hungry Hollow," has been described as the most picturesque village in Grey County. It is nestled in the valley of the Beaver River near its headwaters. Its founder, Edward Horton, (1816-1864) came to the township in 1853 and acquired five hundred acres in the area where Feversham now stands. The town grew up around the dam, the gristmill and the oatmeal mill which Horton established on his property.

This red brick cottage has been artfully painted to add interest to what is essentially a one-storey box structure. The lower four ranks of brick, the window and door voussoirs, and two separated ranks under the eaves have been painted white to add visual liveliness to the exterior. A sturdy porch also adds to the simple charm of this hillside house.

OWEN SOUND

The Bishop House c.1880

836 2nd Avenue West, Owen Sound, Ontario N4K 4M5

IN 1872, MRS. A. J. EARLY, a young widow, arrived in Owen Sound with her daughter Florence, ten years old, and her son William, eight years old. She and her husband William, had previously lived in Norval, Ontario. She came to Owen Sound to be close to her brothers, John and William Miller (the former was the first Treasurer of Owen Sound and the latter was the first Reeve.) William Jr. became an Owen Sound doctor in the 1890's and died in 1906. Florence married Allan Bishop (brother of W. A. Bishop, the father of the famous Billy Bishop) and had six children. They were Annabelle who died of TB, Allan Jr. killed in World War I, Helen, Howard, Edwin and Jean.

In January, 1880 Anna Early bought the property on 2nd Avenue West behind the library for $200 and built her home there. It was occupied by Bishops until one hundred and one years later, 1981, when Jean died.

It is one of the prettiest houses in Owen Sound. Victorian Gothic Revival in style, it is an asymmetrical ell with white, roughcast cladding and forest green wooden trim. Multiple gables, steeply pitched rooflines and a verandah tucked into the ell define its mass. Winsome design touches are the delicate bargeboard with its drop finial in the front gable, the treillage of the verandah and the shaped drip molds over some of the windows.

Although the house is now one of three adjacent houses comprising a Retirement Home, the front and side facades remain, thankfully, completely untouched.

Buchan Manor 1855

862 2nd Avenue East, Owen Sound, Ontario N4K 2G8

THIS GREAT HOUSE has almost always been owned and occupied by Buchans. It was built in 1855 by Walter E. Buchan, an immigrant from Glasgow, Scotland where his father was a wealthy manufacturer. The land, 7/8 of an acre, was a Crown Patent dated May 14, 1855. The property must have been occupied for several years before the Patent was issued as Walter Buchan's family was housed in a brick house probably built in 1853 on the side street (now 111 7th Street East) while the stone house was erected by a contractor named David Binns. The golden limestone, cut and coursed, was quarried from the escarpment on the west side of the city. The outside walls are twenty-seven inches thick and the corner quoining is massive. Double-hung windows were originally glazed in a eight-panes-over-eight-panes configuration. The ceilings on the main floor are thirteen feet high, on the second floor twelve feet high and on the third floor about seven feet high. Timbers used in the construction are hand hewn and the lath handmade. Wooden pegs secure the roof beams.

Inside, wooden shutters were made for the windows to protect the fifteen room house against the possibility of Indian attack. The rumoured escape tunnel running underneath the house, perhaps to the Sydenham River at the bottom of the property, has never been discovered. Local legend has it that an artist was hired to paint the Union Jack on the ceiling of the dining room so that it could be said that the family always dined under the flag of the British Empire. The verandah across the front of the Georgian-style house is considered to be original with the house. It consists of a lattice treillage in three broad arches.

The interior is arranged on the traditional centre hall plan. The kitchen was in the basement and a dumb waiter system was employed to lift the food to the butler's pantry on the main floor.

The present occupant tells the story of Walter Buchan looking upward to the third storey of this massive house as it was being constructed and instructing the contractor to go no higher. It was quite high enough in Buchan's view. This accounts for the upper right-hand window under the south gable being cut off at the corner.

The carriage house is joined to the house by an addition built somewhat later and in beautifully matching stonework. Another small stone building on the property, divided in half, was built as a privy and a garden shed.

Walter Buchan died on February 27th, 1857 soon after the house was built. His wife later married Mr. Frederick T. Wilkes, a mill owner, who had been appointed first Judge for Grey County in 1854. Mary, his daughter, married Grey County Sheriff, Joseph Maughan. It was through such marriages that growing wealth and power in the fledgling community was concentrated within a relatively few families — a sort of Owen Sound "Family Compact."

George Inglis, the only person outside the Buchan family to own the property, bought it in 1879. About twenty years later it was returned to the Buchans thanks to Ewing Cameron, (a son of Walter Buchan's sister, Margaret) who bought it in 1901 for $3000. In 1930 the property passed into the hands of the granddaughters of Walter Ewing Buchan's brother, David Buchan (for twenty-five years Bursar of the University of Toronto). Jane and Katharine lived in Buchan Manor until Jane's death in 1952 and Katharine's in 1978 and for some of that period it was operated as a small inn. Their sister, Norah had married George Sippi from a well-known London, Ontario family. Georgena Rose Buchan Sippi, their daughter, married Mr. John McWilliam in 1942 and, on his retirement after forty-seven years with the Bank of Montreal, the McWilliams came to live permanently in Buchan Manor. Since Georgena McWilliams death in 1981, Mr. McWilliam has continued to reside in Buchan Manor. His daughter, Mrs. Norah Toth, her husband Gordon, and their two children, Katharine and Andrew also live in Owen Sound.

Sheldon Place - The Frost Estate c.1852

333 4th Avenue West, Owen Sound, Ontario N4K 2R8

John Frost (1808-1869) brought his family from Bytown to Sydenham (Owen Sound) in 1845. He considered Bytown no fit place in which to bring up a family because it was populated by the builders of the Rideau Canal, a rough and lawless bunch in his opinion.

The family chronicler, Stanley Richard Frost, has written about the removal of the family from Bytown to Sydenham (Owen Sound Library Collection of Local History). They travelled by way of the Rideau Canal to Kingston, thence by Lake boat to Toronto, up Yonge Street by wagon to Holland Landing, across Lake Simcoe, along the Severn River to Georgian Bay and by another boat to Sydenham. He writes: "The trip across Georgian Bay was stormy. All passengers were battened below decks and as the lumber on the boat filled the hold to within a couple of feet of the deck, it was uncomfortable to say the least. I guess Grandmother thought her time had come, but when she got to Sydenham she was welcomed by the wife of the Indian Agent who embraced her with tears of joy for the population of white women had by her arrival gone up to two!"

John Frost lost no time in making his mark on Sydenham . He opened a general store, then a brickyard, a stone quarry, a tannery and a flour mill. He was made magistrate in 1845 and mayor in 1868.

He found the beautiful site for his stone house by tramping through the woods on the escarpment west of the Sydenham River from Brooke to Inglis Falls and in February 1852 the Crown granted him fifty-one acres (Lots 4 and 5). The house looks over the city to the eastern escarpment and Georgian Bay.

He planned every inch of the structure himself. It is constructed of golden, cut and coursed limestone in the Georgian style with a generous central entrance and large symmetrically placed windows. A monitor lights the attic and four decorated, stone chimneys rise from the hipped roof. In 1908 a broad verandah was added to two sides of the house with a sunroom on the second floor over the centre entrance.

John and Mary Frost had nine children — five boys and four girls. John, the eldest, was educated as a lawyer and was twice mayor of Owen Sound. He was also a writer. His book, *Broken Shackles,* was written under the pseudonym *Glenelg* and published by William Briggs, Toronto in 1889. It relates the stories of

escaped slaves from the United States some of whom were sheltered in a number of modest dwellings on the Frost estate.

Another son, Alfred John was a brilliant lawyer who became County Crown Attorney in 1875 and Master of the Supreme Court in 1885. Tragically, he died of pneumonia at the age of fifty-one after an ice-boating incident on the bay of Owen Sound. His eldest son, also named Alfred John, was a self-taught wizard in the field of mechanics. Perhaps his most remarkable feat was the creation in about 1900 of one of the first gasoline powered automobiles ever built in Canada.

John Frost's youngest son, James A. Frost, inherited Sheldon Place early in the 20th century. His daughter, Catherine, who had lived for many years in England continued the family tradition on the estate from 1942 until her death in 1978 when it finally was sold out of the family. The warmhearted Kitty (Frost) Mitchell played a major role in the social and cultural life of Owen Sound, maintaining the lifestyle of an upper class English woman in her English style country estate located in a provincial Canadian town.

The Frost estate, Sheldon Place, is a treasure not only because it is a grand house on a superb site but because it represents the history of a remarkable family whose humanity and broad interests are in the finest tradition of our country.

JOHN FROST 1808 1880

THE CREASOR HOUSE c.1875

681 4th Avenue West, Owen Sound, Ontario

THIS MASSIVE TWO-STOREY brick house with its distinctive flattened-arch windows is situated on the west escarpment of Owen Sound overlooking the city and the bay to the east. Its steeply pitched roof, gables, two-and-a-half storey bays and the tall, slender proportions of its windows all point to the romantic Gothic-Revival style. Altogether it is an uniquely planned and handsome house on a magnificent property.

The staircases of the interior are built inward from the south wall — the long axis of the house. Staged triple windows light the wide second floor landing. There are eleven rooms in the main house plus a self contained two storey apartment. The seven fireplaces are faced with grey and white marble.

The property, nine acres, first came from the Crown by Patent in 1847 to John McDonald, eventually passing into the hands of David A. Creasor in 1873 who bought a portion of the nine acres for $2200. Presumably the house was built at this time. Creasor was a leading light of Owen Sound, becoming Mayor in 1882-83 and County of Grey Judge in 1891. He died in 1895 and his family moved to Winnipeg about 1900. The new owner in 1938, a Mr. Donaldson, painted the red brick white, wired the house and installed gas heat. The next owner, Dr. George Taylor enclosed the front porch. A self-sufficient apartment was made by a Mr. Copus in 1946. "Bink" McTavish bought the house in 1959 as a concession to his wife. As the reluctant new owner he named the estate "HADERWAY"!

The McNight House c.1890

518 10th Street "A" West, Owen Sound, Ontario N4K 3R6

The lovely property on which this house is built was acquired from the Crown by George Firstbrook in 1846. It lies on the west escarpment of Owen Sound at the end of a cul-de-sac. Expansive lawns and mature trees frame a rambling Victorian house considerably enhanced by a picturesque verandah. The mellow, rosy brick is trimmed with bands of buff brick around the windows and the corners of the walls. The repeating roof lines are hipped and the eaves are wide. A classical dentil moulding at the top of the walls is executed in brick. Tall, decorated, double-flue chimneys add their elegance to this handsome house.

Captain Robert McKnight was born in Ireland in 1837 and died here in 1918. He came to Canada as a young man of nineteen. In 1856 he married Mary McLean and they moved first to Markdale and then to Meaford. He was an unsuccessful Liberal candidate in several provincial and federal elections. But in 1875 he was appointed Registrar of Deeds for this district and held that post for forty-three years. He was vice-president of the Grey and Bruce Loan Co. for twenty-nine years and Captain of Leith Company (No. 3) in the 31st Regiment — then succeeding Col. J.P. Telford as Lt. Colonel of the Regiment. His obituary in the Owen Sound paper read, "He was a great reader and scholar and a conversation with him was an education." He and his wife raised two daughters and three sons, one of whom was lost in the First World War.

THE GEORGE MILLER HOUSE c.1857

1584 7th Avenue East, Owen Sound, Ontario N4K 2Z2

THIS PICTURESQUE COTTAGE on the east side of Owen Sound on a street first known as "Cathcart Street" is one of the first houses built in Owen Sound which is still standing. Recently it has undergone extensive remodeling. It has been reclad, reroofed and reglazed. Although the aged texture and colour of the exterior are gone, the original mass and form remain. We are faced with the question of whether this is a successful compromise between the need to save an historic house and the need of the new owners to evolve the house to suit their requirements.

The broad sweeping front gable roofline with its narrow eaves, highlighted by a Palladian window, the offset bow window and the simple entrance give a certain charm to this unusual cottage which was designed by the first owner himself.

He was George S. Miller, an Irishman born in 1813, as was his wife, Eliza. They came to Owen Sound with their four sons in 1856 from Niagara-on-the-Lake when Miller was offered the job of manager of the grain elevator and warehouse. In 1860 he became harbourmaster, a post he held for forty-five years.

The land on which the house was built was granted by the Crown in 1855 to A. M. Stephens one of Owen Sound's most colourful pioneers. He sold these two lots from his sizable grant two years later to Miller for £200. This transaction illustrates how the very first settlers, who acquired land free from the Crown and then sold it off in city lots were able to quickly amass considerable wealth. They were amply rewarded for their pioneering instincts and foresight.

Photo by Ruth Cathcart

Photo by Ruth Cathcart

THE RIXON HOUSE c.1860

894 5th Avenue East, Owen Sound, Ontario N4K 2R8

THIS TWO STOREY, rough-faced and coursed limestone house is a good example of the Georgian style in this region. Its simple rectangular mass, twice as long as it is wide, is low to the ground. Its colour is golden. Its fenestration is symmetrical and its entrance is recessed. The louvered shutters are designed not just for decoration but for practical purpose as they swing inward on original hinges. The two gable-roof dormers with projecting eaves add interest to the front elevation, and the handsome roof trim displays a moulded fascia and a plain frieze with the eaves returned.

Land Registry records show that the property, one-half acre, was granted by the Crown to the Rev. Joseph W. Robinson in 1856. Five years later he sold the property to the Middlesex Bible Society for £300. Sometime in the 1860's a church was built here called the New Connexion Methodist Church. An 1879 map of Owen Sound shows a new incarnation for the stone building — a public school. Finally in 1888 it became the home of the Rixon family.

Mr. Rixon was born in London, England in 1838, the son of a solicitor. He came to Leith in 1864 where he settled until 1888 when he came to Owen Sound. For several years he sailed on the Lakes, being purser on the *Silver Spray, Campana* and other steamers sailing to Owen Sound. Later he formed a partnership with James Maitland having charge of a wharf and warehouse. His sawmill became known under the name of *The Rixon, Ainslee, Stoddart Company.* Mrs. Rixon was the daughter of Adam and Isabella Ainslie from Leith. "Ainslie Wood" is now a public recreation area.

The interior of the house reflects the simple dignity of the exterior. A flat multipaned transom and sidelights surround a four-paneled door. The staircase rises from the left of the centre hall to a landing which is lit by the second-storey window over the entrance. The rooms with nine foot ceilings are generous in size. Fireplaces are the focus of the front parlour and the dining room. The interior walls are constructed of plaster which is applied to the roughcast covering the solid stone.

A back wing with shiplap cladding was added to the house early on. It contains the kitchen and the maids rooms above.

During the tenure of the Rixon family some decorative and infrastructure changes were made to the interior. The woodwork was grained to resemble oak.

Arches were built between the main rooms downstairs from which velvet hangings were hung. Radiators were installed in the 1920's. Today the simply moulded woodwork including the high baseboards is painted white and the velvet hangings are gone.

Some of the Rixon's Victorian furniture remains however. The walnut extension dining table seats eighteen people. There are Victorian settees, cupboards, occasional tables and a huge mirror measuring seventy-two by fifty inches which has reflected the genteel life of the house over the one hundred and thirty or more years of its existence.

The Eddie Sargent House c.1880

2546 4th Avenue West, Owen Sound, Ontario N4K 4Z2

THIS PICTURESQUE VICTORIAN Gothic-Revival house, named "Green Gables" by Roma Sargent has it all; an ownership history which evokes the past of this region, a beautiful site and a romantic castle-like appearance.

The house is thought to have been built by a John Scagel who bought the property in 1876. He was a merchant whose store on Union street was next door to the Parker & Cattle Drugstore. In 1862 Scagel advertised dry goods, crockery, hardware and "pure liquors" and offered to take some produce in exchange for his goods. His name appears in the *Owen Sound Poetical Directory* of 1863 over this charming bit of doggerel:

"Choose for yourselves, his flooded shelves
Contain our wholesale bill,
Keeps goods homemade, and foreign trade
Of fashion, taste and skill.
Dry goods each class, paints, nails and glass
Rice, sugars, teas in store,
Made-clothing there, boots, shoes, hardware,
And things a thousand more."

The next owner, Benjamin Squire (born 1824), bought the property in 1881 for $2100 and finished the house. His first wife was an Aboriginal woman who bore him two daughters, Mary Ann and Sarah Ann. His second wife Eliza had five children; Norman, Minnie, Edwin, Mabel and Daniel. Two of the little girls shared a tiny bedroom in the tower. They recounted waking in the morning, sometimes to see an Indian encampment below the escarpment on which the house was built. The natives had come to town to sell their basketware to the townspeople. Some days later the encampment would be gone with no sign left that humans had ever occupied that space. They had come silently in the night and left silently before dawn.

Owner number three was Henry Abell who moved to the house from Wolseley, Kepple Township, in 1903. He paid $2300 for the property. Abell was born in Devonshire, England in 1850 and came to Wolseley in 1866 where he and his sons eventually cleared up to three hundred acres of bush, a prodigious feat. He had married Catherine Scott of Oxendon and they raised four sons and a daughter. The sons all became professionals — a doctor, a dentist and two pharmacists. His daughter, Ola May married Robert E. Wilson of Owen Sound. It was said that the Abels used seven stoves to heat this large frame house.

The house was largely derelict when the Sargents acquired it in 1945. Eddie Sargent, a figure of almost mythical proportions in this region, was a one-time mayor of Owen Sound and a long-standing Member of the Provincial Parliament for Grey County.

The house is distinguished by its steeply pitched rooflines, its many gables and its three-storey square tower capped by a widow's walk. It is situated on the edge of the escarpment looking east over Georgian Bay, its street side shielded by mature Norway spruce.

The Kennedy House c.1885

940 1st Avenue West, Owen Sound, Ontario N4K 4K5

THIS HOUSE WAS BUILT on property originally granted by the Crown in 1856 to Walter E. Buchan, the builder of Buchan Manor on 2nd Street East. Matthew Kennedy bought the lot in 1881 and built his Victorian Gothic Revival house soon after.

His father, William Kennedy, came to Canada from Glasgow, Scotland in 1831. He married Agnes Stark in 1837 and Matthew, one of nine children was born in 1845.

The Kennedys, father and older sons, started a planing and matching factory near the Harrison Mill Dam prior to 1857 and, in 1863, opened a millwright business and machine shop. "Wm. Kennedy and Sons" was formed in 1867 and moved in 1884 to 1st Avenue West where it is now known as the "Black, Clawson, Kennedy" factory. Matthew took over the firm when his father died in 1885.

Matthew Kennedy became a pillar of the community. He was, at one time or another, President of the Board of Trade, Mayor of Owen Sound (1895-96), member of the School Board and License Commissioner. It was said of him, "His prosperity was due to energy, enterprise, integrity, intelligence. He operated by the strictest principles of honesty and the progressive spirit which promotes public good." (Grey County and Owen Sound Museum files.)

This brick house, typical for the period in its ell form, retains its original character today despite the removal of the elegant, two-sided porch (shown in the vintage photo), additions to the northern and western elevations and the white painting of the brick. Fortunately, the original, flattened-arch windows with their louvered shutters remain. These windows, the gables and bays and the steeply pitched roofs all provide liveliness and interest to the mass of this large house.

Vintage photo courtesy of the Grey-Owen Sound Museum

The John Wright House c.1895

935 2nd Avenue West, Owen Sound, Ontario N4K 4M8

JEMIMA GRAY WALKER, (1837-1908) and John Wright, (1840-1910) were married in Edinburgh, Scotland in 1861 and came directly to Canada in May of that year. After living briefly in Hamilton, Guelph and Elora, they moved to Owen Sound in 1867 where they resided the rest of their lives. There were two sons, James born in 1864 and William born in 1866. The Wright flour and oatmeal mills were the basis of the family's prosperity. In time John Wright became the president of the Owen Sound Board of Trade and an esteemed town councillor.

The property, first owned by Walter Buchan in 1856, was purchased by John Wright in 1891 for $3250. This splendid three-storey, red brick house has been changed very little over the years, as the circa 1900 photo shows. The house features two towers. Their mansard roofs are pierced by dormer windows with shaped hoods in the French Second Empire style. This style was introduced into Ontario at about the time of Confederation and disappeared completely by the turn of the century. It derived from Paris where Napoleon the III used it extensively in a massive effort to beautify the capital of France.

The recessed entrance, second-storey porch, patterning in the roof shingles (originally), the prominent stone belt courses in the north tower and contrasting window treatments all point to the eclecticism of the period. By this means, a leading citizen could demonstrate to the community that he was indeed someone capable of possessing such a grand house.

Vintage photo above courtesy of the Grey-Owen Sound Museum

THE EATON HOUSE - "EAGLES' NEST" C.1862 (enlarged 1888)

727 4th Avenue West, Owen Sound, Ontario N4K 4V3

THE EATON HOUSE was occupied by the Christopher Eaton family between 1888 and about 1918. Mr. Eaton had established a brewery on Charlotte Street (now at about 778 3rd Ave. West) in the early days of Owen Sound. His retail liquor outlet was at 45 Poulett Street. The nine acre property on the west escarpment of Owen Sound on which his house was built, was transferred as a Patent from the Crown to John Mills in 1847. Mills was Chief Constable for Owen Sound from 1851 to some time in the 1890's. In 1862 it became the property of Joseph Maughan (later to become Sheriff of Grey County) who built a one-storey brick house there. The Eatons bought the house in 1888 and added another storey.

The Georgian style house with three bays has stone quoining and stone window sills and lintels. The roof is hipped and was originally punctuated at the front by a curved-roof dormer. The front entrance is modest with a glazed transom over the door and a porch supported by two pillars and surmounted by a pediment. The interior boasts sixteen rooms including three baths. The ceilings are twelve feet high and the doors are massive. The kitchen, as was common, was located in the lower level and the food was lifted by means of a dumbwaiter to the dining room above. The large sunroom at the rear of the house, overlooking the city and the bay has been called, "The Treehouse" because it is at the level of the treetops. The Eatons closed in a balcony to create the sunroom in 1912. The overall impression given by this structure is one of simple, balanced gravity.

Mrs. Annie Eaton was the daughter of Senator Robert Jaffray, one-time owner and publisher of the Toronto Globe. She was active in the community — working with the Women's Music Club, the Earl Grey Chapter of the I.O.D.E., and the Angelica Shakespeare Club. The Eaton home was a centre for social and recreational activities in Owen Sound. The beautiful garden, sloping downward from the lip of the escarpment was the scene of garden parties, and, when the pond froze in the winter, for skating parties. When their son Jaffray Eaton, went overseas to fight in the First World War, Mrs. Eaton along with Mrs. Harvey the wife of Dr. Richard Harvey of the Medical Corps, opened the *Grey Rooms* at 20 Craven Street in London, England; a building owned by the Toronto Globe. There, servicemen from the Grey-Bruce region could relax and meet their friends.

Jaffray Eaton lost his life in World War I and his father died about 1915. Annie Eaton, bereft of her family, returned to live in Toronto where she died in 1937.

The John MacLean House c.1861

1663 5th Avenue East, Owen Sound, Ontario N4K 2S3

This property was first conveyed by Patent from the Crown to Thomas Scott in September 1861. Scott was Mayor of Owen Sound in 1867 and the first MLA from Grey-North in 1867-75. After holding this property for only a month he sold it to John Maclean. The McLean family lived here for eighty-two years. In 1962 the present owners acquired the property and they are responsible for the meticulous restoration of the house and garden.

John G. Maclean was born at Robertson, Scotland in September 1816. In 1837 he came to Canada and settled in Toronto where he entered into partnership with John Riddell as merchant tailors. In 1857 he retired from business and three years later, in 1860, came to Owen Sound. He married Elizabeth, second daughter of John Blyth and sister of George Blyth of *The Chatsworth News*. Mr. Maclean employed himself in fruit raising and took great interest in horticulture, being a member of the Horticultural Society. In politics he was a staunch Reformer. Their children were William of Victoria, B.C., John of Sault Ste. Marie, Robert B. of Brantford and Misses Grace and Mary.

The construction of this house is unusual. Six inch pine planks were laid flat, one atop the other, with one inch spacers between. Plaster was then applied to both the interior and the exterior. There is lath and plaster in the ceilings. The corners of the walls in the foyer and upstairs landing are curved rather than right-angled, an unusual and handsome variation. The ceiling in the entry is pressed tin. Balusters of the curved staircase are finely turned and the newel post is elegantly simple. The recessed entrance has a fine four-panel door with glazed transom and sidelights.

The house is Neo-Classical in feeling even though it is irregular in mass — a hallmark of the later Picturesque Movement. The ventilating oculus in the gable refers to classicism while the decorative bargeboard looks forward to the Gothic Revival which would become common in about a decade. The roof of the main section of the house is hipped and the gabled section has a fairly steep pitched roof. The windows are double-hung six-over-six panes. A modern bay window has been constructed on the main floor in the gable section of the house and a large sunroom has been added to the rear.

This spacious property is located on the east escarpment of Owen Sound. The grounds are well kept and highlighted by perennial beds, a grove of Norway Spruce and a magnificent yellow magnolia at the front entrance.

THE COLIN RUSSEL HOUSE c.1890

932 3rd Avenue West, Owen Sound, Ontario N4K 4P6

THREE WORDS BEST describe the style of this massive red brick house — late Victorian eclectic. Its outstanding feature is the tower which is capped by a roofline rising from concave to convex. The second storey of the tower is lit by a large Palladian window and the third storey by round-topped windows on all four sides. The design of the house itself includes dentil mouldings under the tower roof, sunrise motifs in two gables, an advancing two-storey bay in the front elevation, a curved two-storey bay on the north, massive decorated chimneys terminating in flared caps and a two-sided porch enhanced by "Aesthetic Period" diagonal spindles. In fact the Oriental flavoured roofline of the tower, the sunrise motif and the porch decoration all refer to the "Aesthetic Period" of the late nineteenth century which incorporated design motifs from foreign cultures, especially that of Japan.

The house was built between about 1890 and 1900 by John W. Redfern who, in 1869, had established a hardware, sheet metal and plumbing business on main street known as *Redfern & Lepan.* He sold the house to Owen Sound Police Magistrate David Creasor in about 1908 for $6,000. Creasor rented the building as a residence and office for the American Consul, Augustus G. Seyfert. Owen Sound had full consular status from 1879 to 1915. After only a year the consulate moved to 908 2nd Avenue East where it remained until 1915 when it was moved to Fort William and Prince Arthur at the head of Lake Superior.

From 1937 until 1989 the property belonged to the Colin Russel family. Russel Bros. was a large metal fabrication and boat building company in Owen Sound which prospered originally by building tugboats for the lumbering trade.

THE ALEXANDER M. STEPHENS HOUSE c.1855

1623 6th Avenue East, Owen Sound, Ontario N4K 2V6

THIS TWO STOREY, coursed stone Georgian-style house with prominent quoining sits four-square on the property. Its symmetrically placed windows with stone lug sills and slab lintels, its fine doorway with transom and sidelights, and its truncated hipped roof all lend a feeling of permanence and prosperity to the house. Stephens acquired the land, four-fifths of an acre, from the Crown in October 1854.

In the early winter of 1840 Alexander Stephens, only 19 years old, worked on a crew of twelve to open the Garafraxa Road — from Arthur to the mouth of the Sydenham River — making about four miles each day. This young fellow decided he loved the challenge and excitement of the life of a frontiersman and returned to Sydenham, as Owen Sound was then called, in the spring of 1842 to stay. Eventually his brothers and sister would follow; all to make major contributions to the life of the young community. One brother, W.A. Stephens, became one of Canada's first published poets and was mayor of Owen Sound in 1867. His sister Mary, who married the prominent entrepreneur R. J. Doyle, established a private school in town and was one of the founders of the W.C.T.U. in Canada (The Women's Christian Temperance Union).

In his memoir published in 1870, *The Early Days of Owen Sound,* Alexander Stephens recounts his experiences clearing roads, building bridges, sailing the fifteen ton schooner "Fly" to move goods to and from Owen Sound, and transporting fish overland for sale in the south. He describes some of the early pioneers of Grey County, the land grab in Euphrasia and Collingwood Townships and the over logging of the forests which commenced soon after the settlement of the land.

Stephens served on the town council from 1860 to 1880 and was mayor in 1865-66 and in 1872.

THE URQUART HOUSE c.1858

745 2nd Avenue West, Owen Sound, Ontario N4K 2M2

THIS ONE-STOREY, roughcast "Ontario Cottage," a vernacular version of the English Regency cottage, is set well back from 2nd Avenue West on a lovely site bordering the Sydenham River. Its central entrance with glazed transom and sidelights oriented to the central hall and square floor plan, double hung windows of six-panes-over-six and medium hipped roof, all bespeak the style of the Colonist-Regency house built as a rational personal environment in a new and untamed country. The four large well-lit rooms, two on either side of the spacious hall, create a feeling of harmony and rest. Originally they were likely to have been the parlour, dining room and two bedrooms. The house is raised from the ground by a stone cellar which would have accommodated the kitchen and staff quarters, a sensible adaptation in a country with extremes of climate.

Land Registry records show that the land was granted to a James Fryle in 1853. In 1855 ownership passed to the redoubtable Walter Ewing Buchan of Buchan Manor and was then mortgaged in 1858 by Buchan's widow, Ann. This suggests the date of the building of the house. The wood mouldings of the doors and windows would also suggest the late 1850s date of construction as they closely resemble in profile the mouldings of several other houses confirmed to have been built at that time in Sydenham (Owen Sound).

In 1880, Donald P. Urquhart, a successful merchant in groceries, acquired the property and it remained in this family until 1974.

PROTON TOWNSHIP

THE NOBLE/ROBINSON HOUSE c.1890

Proton Township Lot 228 Con 1 (Old Survey)

IT IS NOT KNOWN whether Edward Noble built this house when the land was in his possession from 1855 to 1892, or whether his successor, Thomas Robinson, built it soon after he bought the property from Noble. Whatever the case, the house remains as a quintessential example of "Ontario Gothic" and is well-known to passersby on the Toronto-Sydenham Road just north of Dundalk (now Highway 10).

Many of the characteristics of the Gothic Revival style are seen here — polychromatic brickwork, heightened elevation to accommodate an upper half-storey, steeply pitched roof and, above all, a centre-front gable trimmed with gingerbread.

Fortunately, this house retains its original verandah with a gently curved awning or bell-cast roof which is supported by slender posts and decorated with lacy gingerbread. These verandah roofs have almost all disappeared from our landscape. This example is a reminder of what we have lost.

The Manse c.1912

Proton Township Part Lot 5 Con 4 (in the hamlet of Cedarville)

LOCAL HISTORIAN JAMES FEAIRS has written in his *Historical Notes Leading Up To The Centennial Anniversary of Morrison Church Cedarville,* "John Morrison came to Cedarville as a student missionary in the summer of 1861. At the end of theological training in Knox College, he returned to the Proton congregation, they having petitioned Presbytery to have him return." Thus began the saga of a devoted clergyman and his flock. Morrison, born in the Hebrides off the west coast of Scotland, was a man who was loved and admired by all the pioneer families of Proton Township because he served them so faithfully. The fine brick church built in 1900 was named Morrison church in tribute to him.

Next door, in 1912, the congregation built a manse. It is a simple but handsome house with vestigial brackets under its wide eaves and a crested dormer to give light to the attic. A centre front door in the second-storey, at one time, gave out onto a balcony which was supported by the charming porch below.

THE CAMPBELL/SUDDEN HOUSE c.1900

Dundalk (91 Victoria St.) Plan 480 Blk Pt lot 4 RPR3349 Part 1

IN 1896 DUGALD CAMPBELL (1869-1953) came to Dundalk and purchased a drug store which he operated until 1910. After an absence of eight years he returned to Dundalk where he worked as a druggist until the early 1930's and then in his own optical business until his death. In 1953 Dr. Stanley Clifford Sudden, who had practiced dentistry in Dundalk since 1923, bought the Campbell house where he practiced until his retirement in 1968. Sudden was a public-spirited man who served on school and church boards and promoted hockey and baseball in the area.

The house is said to be modeled after one which Dugald Campbell admired in the affluent neighbourhood of Rosedale in Toronto. This Dutch gabled style is highly unusual in Grey County as is the parapet top of the bay window. By such means a "touch of class" has been added to the otherwise square, two-storey red brick house of a type built in quantity in this region in the first quarter of the twentieth century.

The R.J. Doyle Jr. House c.1893

Sarawak Township Lot 15 Con 3

RICHARD JUDSON DOYLE (1834-1903) was born in Nova Scotia. He came to Owen Sound as a young man and married Mary Stephens, sister Of A. M. Stephens and W. A. Stephens, both prominent figures in the history of the town.

Doyle's industry and initiative seemed to know no bounds. He was an inventor with many patents to his name. He was vitally interested in politics and was an astute business man. He and his wife were staunch prohibitionists. She founded the first chapter in Canada of the WCTU, the Women's Christian Temperance Union. Their daughters, Winnie and Eva, operated the Seldon House in Owen Sound as a "Temperance Hotel." Mary Stephens Doyle also founded a private school in Owen Sound.

Doyle purchased the site of the town of Dundalk from the government and during the building of The Toronto, Grey and Bruce Railway, laid it out as a town plot. He also had extensive contracts in wood for the railway. He established works for the manufacture of fruit barrels, the design of which he patented. He founded The Dominion Grange Mutual Fire Insurance Co. and the official Grange paper, *The Grange Bulletin,* later named *The Co-Operator and Patron.*

In 1879 Mr. Doyle purchased Shallow Lake from the government and, with the financial assistance of the province and the municipality, reclaimed a large section of the lake. One hundred thousand dollars was subscribed by fellow businessmen in Owen Sound who formed the North American Chemical, Mining and Manufacturing Company. The long, difficult process of developing a viable cement product was begun. Doyle himself experimented with the burning of marl from the lake bed in a brick kiln fired with coal which he built on his own property near Balmy Beach.

Eventually the partnership disintegrated and one of the partners, R.P. Butchart went on to form the Owen Sound Portland Cement Company, Shallow Lake. Andrew Armitage, author of *The Bruce Peninsula Explorer,* has written, "In Owen Sound and the cities of southwest Ontario, in Toronto, Ottawa and Montreal, the clay and marl of the small dry lake that gave the village its name, built dams and docks, office and government buildings, roads and bridges." *The Scientific American* gave Doyle credit for being the first man on the continent of North America to manufacture Portland cement from native marl. He also won awards from the Paris and Philadelphia Expositions for the best firebrick and the best fireproof paint produced at that time.

He served on the council and as Reeve of Sarawak for many years.

Longtime residents, Walter Beattie and Harold Graham, reflect in their book *Brooke* edited by Melba Croft, on the influence of the great R. J. Doyle, by recounting this anecdote. Doyle arrived at the Brooke train station precisely on time for his train. However the train had left the station a minute or two early. The station master was required to contact Park Head, the next stop, and have the train backed up to Brooke to pick up its very important passenger!

In the last years of his life he spent the winters on his six hundred acre plantation in Florida. He died at home in October, 1903.

This Queen Ann style house was built by his son, R. J. Doyle Jr. in 1893 on the family property just north of Owen Sound. It is situated on the escarpment overlooking the bay and is fronted by a apple orchard. After all, in addition to his myriad interests and skills, R.J. Doyle was a keen orchardist.

THE VEITCH/CAVELL COTTAGE c.1860

Sarawak Township Lot 31 Con 2

ROSE MACLEOD, IN her charming book, *Sarawak Saga,* wrote (page 309), "Sarawak has an old landmark in the form of a dear little old stone cottage situated on Scott's Hill. It is so old, no one can remember the year in which it was built." She tells the story of a prank played on a later owner. A couple of his friends, in his absence, along the whole side of the cottage, painted the words, "Upstairs girl wanted." The owner, as amused as the rest of the community, left the message there for many years.

Land Registry records show that Thomas Veitch acquired the Patent to his one hundred acres in October, 1888 but it is thought that his house was built much earlier. In December, 1922 he sold his property to Fred Cavell for $2,000 and it remained in that family for many years.

The twenty-four by twenty-eight foot cottage is constructed of hand hewn wall studs and ceiling beams, and stone walls two feet thick. The front facade and the lower part of the side walls are made of beautifully coloured stones of a variety of shapes and sizes, roughly coursed. The rest of the cottage is stone rubble work. Its situation on a height of land gives this charmer an air of insouciance and command.

ROYSTON PARK c.1875

Sarawak Township Lots 10,11 Con 3

LOCAL HISTORY HAS it that this two storey rubble stone house was built as the servants' quarters and kitchen for a much larger structure which was never accomplished because of lack of funds. This would account for the abruptly finished east elevation. Whatever the case, it is a large, solid house of distinction.

The first owner, William Roy from Scotland, obtained the land in 1863. His house was built in the mid 1870's from stone found on the property. He and his wife Jessie, who was an acclaimed amateur botanist, imported seedlings of Scotch pine and spruce to beautify their property. They played host to many Canadian field naturalists according to Andrew Armitage, author of *The Bruce Peninsula Explorer,* 1994. Armitage writes, "Jessie and her botanizing friends collected rare plants in Sarawak and Keppel and up the Peninsula. It wasn't unusual during the 1870's for Mrs. Roy to send large crates of pressed plants — ferns, mosses, sedges, and wildflowers — to museums in Europe and the United States."

In 1896 the property was sold to William Morrison Sr. who replaced the burned-out barn with a magnificent double-hipped-roof structure. His son, William Morrison Jr. built a large greenhouse on the property and went into the nursery business. The Turner family has farmed here since 1920.

SAUNDERS/LEE FARMHOUSE 1882 (date stone)

Sarawak Township Pt Lot 20 Con 1

THIS FARMHOUSE, BUILT of cut and coursed fieldstone (referred to as "hard heads" by local residents), is typical of house design of the 1880's in this region. If we approach the right side elevation shown in this photograph, the impression is of an earlier generic style referred to as "Georgian." This elevation has a centre door and symmetrically placed windows under a pitched roof. However, the real front elevation exhibits picturesque elements of the Gothic Revival style such as asymmetrical mass, several gables and various rooflines, a verandah, and the generic pointed arch window. The house is nestled under the Niagara Escarpment.

William Saunders was born in Scotland in 1828 and came to Grey County in 1856. The land was granted to him by the Crown in May, 1875 and the house was built in 1882. He and his wife, Jean Clark, raised six children. Their son, William Saunders Jr., his wife Ada Matthews, and their two children continued to live and farm here until 1940 when the property was sold to the Frank George Lee family. The present owners are Wayne and Carol Lee with their two sons Robert and Randy.

THE THOMAS CAVERS HOUSE c.1875

Sarawak Township Pt Lot 19 Con 1

THE PATENT FROM the Crown for this one hundred acre farm was given to Thomas Elliott in April 1872. Three years later he sold the property to Thomas Cavers who built this fine fieldstone house. Of particular note are the large windows, the doorway with its transom and sidelights — all surmounted by stone slab lintels. A rubble stone extension at the rear gives this house an overall tee conformation. It is common knowledge in the community that the stonemason's fee was a yoke of oxen.

The house is sheltered under the Niagara Escarpment and looks eastward toward the "sound" of Owen Sound.

Sarawak Township has the distinction of being the smallest township in Ontario. Its area is only sixteen square miles. It was inhabited by the Newash Indians until 1857 when a government treaty moved them north to the Cape Croker Reservation. In return for their giving up the land the Indians were each promised an annuity, frame houses equal to those they were leaving, and a new church with a burial ground.

ST. VINCENT TOWNSHIP

THE JOHN WHITE HOUSE c.1860

St. Vincent Township N 1/2 Lot 5 Con 10

HERE IS A HANDSOME, two-storey, solid brick house in the Georgian style with an impressive entrance and the original glazing in the lower front windows. The eaves are returned in the gable ends of the roof and the fascia is decorated with dentil mouldings. The brick work is unusual for this region, being a Flemish Bond on the front elevation and a variation of Common Bond on the sides. Raised bricks at the corners are painted white for emphasis, in the Victorian manner.

The land was patented in 1851 in the name of William Osborne. In the same year John White paid £100 for the one hundred acres and mortgaged it for £75. It is possible that the house was built by 1860. The style is consistent with this period of domestic architecture in this region.

c.1867

St. Vincent Township Pt. Lot 28 Con 6

HERE IS AN EARLY fieldstone house which narrowly escaped destruction by the Federal government in its expropriation of land in St. Vincent Township for the Meaford Tank Range in 1942. More than one quarter of St. Vincent was taken over by the Department of Defense — seventeen thousand acres of land. Those families who lost their farms still harbour resentment against the government on account of the land grab. This farm stands just outside the perimeter of the Tank Range. The house is a reminder of others which were lost.

On June 3, 1852 David Layton received this two hundred acre lot from the Crown. He mortgaged his property in 1859 and in 1861. It was sold to Charles Lister in 1867 for $2500. The house would have been built by either Layton or Lister sometime in the 1860's. David Layton served on the first full St. Vincent Township Council in 1851.

The siting of this house has much to do with its appeal. It is set well back from the road and framed by mature trees and shrubs. The "gothic" or front bay is well-proportioned as is the one-storey stone addition.

The Free House c.1855

St. Vincent Township Lot 1 Con 9

Here is a simply beautiful and sensitively restored early limestone house, with extensive modern additions to the rear. The glowing stone has been carefully cut and fitted in the front elevation. The stonework of the side elevations is more random. The quoins, sills and lintels are cut from a contrasting lighter shade of stone. The doorway is slightly recessed, always a good idea in this northern climate. The cornice is boldly moulded and the roof eaves returned. The house is small — only one and a half storeys — but it is entirely pleasing because of its simplicity and its authenticity.

Registry records show that the two hundred acre lot was patented to George Manhart in 1844 but three years later it was sold for £10 to Henry Free (1824-1888) who had married an Ann Pearce. A brother, William Pakenham Free (1829-1896) bought the south half of the farm for £50 in 1852 and a Richard Free was willed the north half in 1888.

The James Storey House c.1860

St. Vincent Township North Part Lot 5 Con 9

JAMES STOREY (1809-1896) received the Patent from the Crown for his two hundred acres December 16, 1839 the year he married Esther Free (1821-1896). He had come to the new world from Roxburghshire, Scotland. Their children were Ann, William, Henry, Esther and Mary Jane. In 1881 James willed the north and south halves of the farm to his sons, Henry and William and the land continued in the Storey family until the early 1960's.

The house stands on a height of land looking eastward. Nearby is a "dry stone fence" (an unmortared stone wall) one hundred and twenty rods in length, said to be one of only two such fences in Grey County. The house is typical of the solid cut and coursed stone houses built by and for Scottish immigrants to Grey County. It stands to demonstrate to the community that this family had prospered, that they were dependable, foursquare people who valued a carefully organized and hardworking lifestyle.

SULLIVAN TOWNSHIP

The Parsonage of St. Peter's Lutheran Church

1874 (date stone)

Sullivan Township   Lot 18 Con 7

THE ORIGINAL MEMBERS of this Lutheran congregation came north to Sullivan Township from the area around Preston (now Cambridge) in the late 1850's. Their first services of worship were held in 1862 in their own homes. In 1865 a log church was built and in 1874, this parsonage. The adjoining church was built in 1881. The pretty closed porch was added to the parsonage in 1893.

The random-size stones of the house are roughly laid in rows, or courses. Larger stones are used over the windows and at the corners of the house. The felicitous combination of a rather severe three-bay stone house with a fanciful Victorian wooden porch built almost twenty years later, draws this house quite out of the ordinary.

The Robert McEwen House c.1880

Sullivan Township Pt Lot 1 Con 3

ROBERT MCEWEN WAS born near Ottawa in 1830. When he was seventeen years old he came to Sydenham (Owen Sound) and worked at Boyd's Wharf until he had saved enough money to buy two hundred acres of bush at one dollar an acre to add to the forty acre grant he received in 1856 from the Crown. In those early years both Methodist and Presbyterian services of worship were held in his log house.

He married Jane Shouldice and they had twelve children, one of whom, Andrew, continued the operation of the farm. His son, Wilmer McEwen succeeded him. *The History of Sullivan Township 1858-1975 Volume 1* (page 272) tells how, in the early days, the McEwens drove their cattle one hundred and twenty miles to Toronto in order to sell them to the butchers there. There is also this revealing tale. "John McEwen told of one time when he was eighteen and his brother Leonard sixteen. They wanted to go to Owen Sound, a distance of thirteen miles, to see the Volunteers on the 24th of May. Their father did not want them to go as there was much work to be done so, as they were going against his wish, he only gave them ten cents each for spending money. Leonard spent his ten cents, but John wouldn't use his, even though he had nothing to eat all day in Owen Sound. He gave the money back to his father and he took it too."

The one and a half-storey frame house commands expansive views over the rolling landscape. It is designed to include the usual vocabulary of patterned brickwork, central gable over the entrance and a decorative verandah across the front of the house. Over the years many of these verandahs have been removed, sadly. They were built not only for the embellishment of the front facade but because they broke the undue height of such houses. They also provided a clean, dry place where the long-skirted ladies of the house took the air.

The Patrick Kelly House 1862

Sullivan Township W Pt Lot 7 Con 2

PATRICK KELLY RECEIVED the Patents from the Crown to the west and east parts of Concession 2 (one hundred and five acres) in 1855 and 1856. This land remained in the family name until 1947. The earliest Census of Sullivan Township in 1851 shows that the Kelly family; Patrick thirty years, Catherine twenty-seven years, James three years, and Hanna one year, had already occupied the land for at least four years before receiving the Patent. During that time they would have fulfilled their settlement duty of clearing and placing under crop, one third of the property.

The following information was found written on a board under the main staircase:

"This stone house was erected on lot no. 7, 2nd concession of Sullivan County of Grey Canada West in the year 1862 for Patrick Kelly the grantee of the said lot and his wife Catherine Godfrey both being native of Ireland. The names of his children are James the eldest aged 13, Hannah aged 11, John aged 8, Michael aged 7, Bob or Patrick aged 5, Mary Ann aged 3, William aged 6 months born during the erection of this building. The mason work was built by General James McMahan a Dundee Irishman. The stone cutting was done by Mr. John Dobbie who lives on the 4 lot south. The carpenter work was done by Mr. James Kelly and his son William Scotchmen of Southhampton."

Their vernacular Georgian cottage is well sited, on the edge of a declivity, with the land falling away behind and to one side of it. This made it possible for the rear of the house to be two and a half-storeys in height while the front elevation is one and a half-storeys in height. The front entrance is well recessed, a relatively uncommon but eminently practical design element in this region of cold, snowy winters. The double hung sashes have six-panes-over-six and the centre hall is lit by a transom and sidelights around the door. Two interior chimneys rise from either end of the gable roof. The stone walls are two feet thick and the ceilings on the main floor are ten feet in height. The kitchen is located in the basement. A few very dark coloured stones give this handsome limestone house a curious lighthearted appearance.

SYDENHAM TOWNSHIP

Bayside Farm - The Rutherford House 1852

Sydenham Township Lot 35 Con A

THOMAS RUTHERFORD WAS appointed by Land Agent John Telfer in the year 1840 to be Purveyor of Government Stores in Sydenham (now Owen Sound). Settlers were beginning to arrive; first by water via Georgian Bay and then via the newly opened Garafraxa Road from Galt. They needed provisions to tide them over until they could supply their own food.

Rutherford (1812-1879) had come from Roxburghshire to Canada when he was twenty-two years old. He first settled in Galt but like so many who were to follow him, he soon came farther north for land. He was the first white settler in Sydenham. He added to his stake by running a hotel on Union Street in Sydenham between 1842 and 1845. In 1844 he married Catherine MacGregor whose family had come to Canada from Perthshire, Scotland in 1841. When the Crown put the land in Sydenham Township up for sale he travelled to Guelph and bought his one hundred acres for £45. The original deed of January 9, 1846 signed by Governor General Charles Murray Cathcart is still in the family's possession.

His character is described by Allan H. Ross in *Reminiscences of North Sydenham,* page 210, "While he made no pretensions to either brilliant gifts or accomplishments Mr. Rutherford was a man of remarkably sound judgement and level headed Scottish sagacity."

Son Malcolm (1854-1938) took over the farm to raise beef cattle and sheep on his father's death. Then in 1919 after serving in World War I, his son Brigadier-General Thomas John Rutherford (1893-1975) assumed responsibility for the farm. T. J. Rutherford had a distinguished career as a soldier and as a farmer. He became Commander of the Grey Regiment (31st) in 1914 and served in France and Belgium in the 4th Canadian Mounted Rifles. After World War I he married Helen Sibbald, helped raise their four children and established a model farm where he bred Registered Dual Purpose Shorthorn cattle. In 1936 he was appointed Sheriff of Grey County.

He returned to his other profession with the advent of the Second World War as Colonel of the Grey and Simcoe Foresters, becoming Brigadier to Command the First Canadian Armoured Brigade. After the war he became the Director of the Soldier Settlement and Veterans' Land Act and later, the first chairman of the Farm Credit Corporation.

Happily, the farm continues in the Rutherford family under the auspices of his son Jaffray, born in 1920, a Bachelor of Science graduate from the Ontario Agricultural College at Guelph. He and his wife, Betty Cumming and their four children operated a dairy and then a beef farm. Jaffray was the first winner of the Tommy Cooper Award in 1959. In 1996 the farm will have been in the Rutherford family for 150 years.

The house is as distinguished by its architecture as by its ownership history — a solid brick vernacular Georgian. The large windows are glazed in the traditional pattern of six-panes-over six-panes. The centre hall is lit by transom and sidelights around the handsome four-paneled door. The massive verandah and upper balcony were added about 1924.

Five generations of Rutherfords whose good characters and skills have enriched Grey County and Canada are descended from that Scottish boy, Thomas Rutherford and his partner and equal, Catherine MacGregor who had the imagination and the tenacity to become settlers in a new land.

CATHERINE RUTHERFORD

THOMAS RUTHERFORD

BRIGADIER-GENERAL
THOMAS JOHN RUTHERFORD, C.B.E., E.D.

THE WILLIAM PATTISON TELFORD HOUSE c.1858

Sydenham Township Part Lots 35 & 36 Con B

BORN IN 1797 OF Scottish parents from Roxburghshire, Scotland, W. P. Telford developed into a man of many gifts. He attended lectures in Edinburgh and qualified as a teacher. He was an accomplished flutist and an ardent fisherman. Five years after marrying Elizabeth Murray in 1835, he and his family emigrated to Canada. They landed in New York and travelled overland to Galt where he continued his teaching career for eight years.

He developed expertise in architectural draughtmanship and woodworking which, added to his other talents as teacher and musician, made him a valuable member of the community of Annan in Sydenham Township to which he migrated in 1848. He died at the age of eighty-two leaving behind memories of a stern but beloved teacher, a man of free and easy hospitality, a talented, industrious woodworker, and a beloved husband and father.

One of the eight of his children who survived infancy, William P. Telford II, taught in his father's school for fourteen years and then went on to various business enterprises in Owen Sound. He managed the Sydenham Mutual Fire Insurance Co., established a private banking firm, Telford & Co. which he sold in 1906 to the Sovereign Bank of Toronto and he was one of the founders in 1889, of the Grey Bruce Loan Co. He became the Liberal Member of Parliament for North Grey for the term 1904-08. Another son, Colonel James P. Telford is described on page 218.

The front facade of W. P. Telford's stone cottage is composed of large and small, squared fieldstones with single stone sills and lintels in the door and window openings. The sparkling red, grey, buff and brown hues of the stone, along with its texture create a visual interest unmatched by any other building material. Sydenham Township can boast of dozens and dozens of these matchless houses.

A twentieth century owner of this property had a frame addition made to the Telford house in which a studio was provided for friend and painter A. Y. Jackson. The front of the long rectangle of the house looks onto an extensive apple orchard while the other side enjoys a view of the bay of Owen Sound with the Niagara escarpment beyond.

THE JAMES P. TELFORD HOUSE c.1865

Sydenham Township Village of Annan Lot 5 Plan 549

THIS HOUSE, BUILT about 1865 by James P. Telford (1839-1933), makes an interesting contrast between Neo-Classic Ontario domestic architecture and the Picturesque style, embodied in the cottage built only a few miles away in 1858 by his father (page 217). The earlier house gives the appearance of lower mass. Its entrance is recessed and offset. Its siting is romantic in that it is far back from the road and takes advantage of a view over the water. The later house is symmetrical in design with Classical Revival details, such as the pediment-shaped front gable and prominent quoining, both of which became standard design elements in Ontario domestic architecture.

Colonel James P. Telford was apprenticed as a blacksmith to James Brown in the village of Sydenham (Owen Sound). With his brother, William P. Telford, he built this house and a smithy in the rear where he served the farmers of the district for the next twenty-five years. The front fence and gate on this property is a lovely example of his work.

He married Catherine MacDonald in 1868 and they raised eight children.

Colonel Telford served in the Canadian militia for thirty-seven years and eventually commanded the 31st Grey Regiment (1894-1900).

In 1887 he sold his blacksmith business and moved to Owen Sound to join the office of The Telford Company and later the Grey Bruce Loan Company.

THE ANDREW SIBBALD HOUSE c.1855

Sydenham Township Lot 25 Con 6

"HE WAS AN UPRIGHT and a conscientious man whose private life was always most exemplary, and his family, one of the most widely known in Sydenham, all followed faithfully in his footsteps." So wrote Allan Ross of Andrew Sibbald in his admirable book, *Reminiscenses of North Sydenham* (page 207).

The stalwart Sibbald was born in Selkirkshire, Scotland in 1816. He came to Canada in 1845 and, like so many other lowland Scots, he settled in Galt. Four years later he migrated northward to Sydenham Township to prove up the land which had just been opened for settlement. He became a successful farmer and played an active role in the community. He also organized the Sydenham Mutual Fire Insurance Company. His life ended in 1886 in his seventieth year.

His stone house is a particularly felicitous example of such houses in Sydenham. The mortar lines between the stones are raised, catching the light. The colours of the stone are warm and lustrous. The large windows extend low to the ground. Two internal stone chimneys bracket the gently pitched roof.

Even though the house was left empty for twenty-five years between 1940 and 1965, it remained as square and solid as it was the day it was built. It has since been refurbished and is an ornament to the community.

Bothwell Manor 1886

Sydenham Township Lot 19 Con 10

THIS HOUSE IS designed in the style known as "Second Empire" — a style which first appeared in Paris in the 1840's when Napoleon III rebuilt the entire centre of the city. In doing so a visual unity was achieved which contributes largely to the beauty for which Paris is acclaimed.

The style was primarily marked by the mansard roof, named for a 17th century French architect, François Mansart. It was designed to provide more space in the upper storey of a building.

This pronounced architectural style first came to Canada, mainly via the United States, at about the time of Confederation. It was widely used for official buildings such as government offices and banks because it made a statement of prosperity and solidity. In domestic architecture, the opulence of the style made it popular with the wealthy and influential as visual proof of their status in the community.

Bothwell Manor is one of the few houses in this region attributed to an architect; George Staples of Owen Sound. Carefully kept family records also record that the contractor was George Suter, the finishing contractor was John Middlebro, the plasterer was a Mr. McLelland and the painter was a Mr. Richards.

The upsurging roofline of the tower is typical of American examples of Second Empire domestic architecture. Perhaps American pattern books were available to the Owen Sound architect. The tower was capped with a glazed belvedere which has since been closed in.

Ornamentation is found in the elaborate roof cornice with its sculptured brackets, moulded double-flue chimneys, polychromatic brickwork, patterning in the roof tiles and iron cresting on the belvedere. The original verandah, a Victorian confection on either side of the projecting centre bay, supported balconies above. It was replaced by the present verandah in 1925.

Hugh Gunn Campbell bought the land from the Crown in 1846 for £80. He built a nine room log house and cleared fifteen acres before selling the property in 1862 for the huge sum of $4000 to John Bothwell. Bothwell (1828-1896) was born and raised on Wimblehill Farm near Kintore, Scotland. When he was seventeen years of age he bound himself to a dry goods merchant in Glasgow in order to become a draper. He emigrated to St. John's, Newfoundland at the age of twenty-four. After three years he came west, first to Sharon and then to Pickering where he opened a business and held the position of postmaster. In 1859 he came to Owen Sound and again went into business. When his shop burned down in 1862 he came here to Sydenham Township to farm and raise his family.

In 1886 the present thirty-six by forty foot house was built. The lower two storeys are of solid brick thirteen inches thick. The cellar is nine feet high. Spring water is gravity fed to the house through a pipe from a range of rock a mile east.

The Walter Aitken House 1868

Sydenham Township Lot 30 (SW Half) Con B

WALTER AITKEN (1812-1897) was born in Hawick, Roxburghshire and came to Galt, Canada in about 1839. On the same ship were forty-five other immigrants from Hawick, one of whom would become his wife. He has been described as standing over six feet in height and as the possessor of a roguish sense of humour. Allan Ross in his *Reminiscenses of North Sydenham* wrote (page 233), "His keenest witticisms were delivered with such a preternaturally grave countenance that one would suppose he were the chief mourner at a funeral, instead of an inveterate fun maker who was enjoying the joke fully as much or more than his listeners were."

He settled in Sydenham Township on Crown land in November 1848 and bought the adjoining fifty acres in 1851. His house, built in 1867-68, is utterly simple; enlivened by the rich colours of the stone and a curious little arched window over the doorway.

Today, Walter Aitken's great great granddaughter, Margaret Miller, and her family reside in this appealing old stone cottage.

Photo by Ruth Cathcart

COUPER'S BRAE FARM c.1855

Sydenham Township Part Lots 22 & 23 Con 7

JOHN COUPER (1819-1896) was born on a farm just west of Glasgow in Renfrewshire. When he was twenty-five years of age he came to Galt, like so many of his fellow lowlanders, and worked for several years before coming north to Sydenham to take up land from the Crown — in his case in 1847. Here he and his wife raised two sons and three daughters. He became a successful farmer and developed a keen interest in local affairs, serving as Councillor and Reeve of the Township. He contested the first provincial election after Confederation as a Liberal, losing to his Conservative opponent.

The field stones of his house have been squared and carefully placed in a pleasing design of colours and shapes. Monochromatic, dressed stone was used in the quoins, lintels, sills and chimneys. The front gable, capped by a finial, is highlighted by a pointed arch window and trimmed with a petticoat of bargeboard. Both finial and bargeboard are likely later additions as are certainly the shaped pediment wood trim around the door and the bay window on one side of the house. The smokehouse attached to the rear of the stone summer kitchen was, at some time, enlarged by the addition of a double brick second storey to make a four room house for hired hands and their families.

THE GIDEON HARKNESS HOUSE c.1860

Sydenham Township Lot 32 Con B

THE BUILDER OF THIS house must have been a stonemason. Who else would have constructed its later additions of stone rather than wood?

In fact, Gideon Harkness (1818-1895) was trained in stonemasonry in Hawick, Roxburghshire, Scotland and after he came to Sydenham Township in about 1844 he constructed several stone houses in the district. He was also a farmer who took a special interest in stock breeding and did much to raise the standard of cattle animal husbandry in the township.

This house represents in stone the plain, solid, no-nonsense attributes of the 19th century lowland Scot. No effort is expended on frills. Function completely controls design. But the colour and texture of the building material and the magnificent siting of the house which overlooks Georgian Bay, gloriously mitigate its stolid design.

THE JAMES GIBSON HOUSE c.1868

Sydenham Township Concession Broken Front Pt Lot 17

JAMES GIBSON (1805-1894) is remembered by Allan Ross, the exemplary chronicler of North Sydenham, as "the finest type of Scottish gentleman of the old school." (*Reminiscenses of North Sydenham*, page 220). He is described as a well educated and talented man of religious conviction, civility and kindness.

He was a cabinetmaker and architect who came from Carstairs, Lanarkshire first to Toronto in 1841 where he designed and built houses. In 1852 he migrated to a farmstead of two hundred acres in Sydenham Township with his wife and four sons, which in due time was cleared and this large stone house was built.

In 1940 the Rev. Donald Campbell McGregor and his wife, Mary (Miller) retired to this house. She had gained national prominence writing under the nom de plume of Marian Keith. Her first novel, *Duncan Polite,* appeared in 1906 and she continued to write fiction almost until her death in 1961. Her publisher, McClelland and Stewart Ltd. is said to have remarked that she was adept at writing in spare moments snatched throughout the day because she put her home and church duties first in her life. She and Lucy Maude Montgomery, both Canadian writers married to clergymen, had much in common. One wonders if they had ever come across Virginia Wolfe's book, *A Room of One's Own.*

The house demonstrates niceties of design not found in other stone houses of the region. The stone quoins rise to shaped capitals at the roof. Slab stone surrounds the windows. The chimney rises flush from the side wall there being no side eaves. And the stonework of the front facade is meticulously cut and coursed. The one storey stone tail of the house forming an overall tee configuration, if indeed it was built by him, is Gibson's only concession to "modern" local ideas of design.

THE LUNN/ROSS HOUSE c.1860

Sydenham Township Lot 29 Con A

THIS PROPERTY OF ONE hundred acres was one of the first settled in Sydenham. Thomas Lunn, from Lilliesleaf, Roxburghshire, Scotland came here in 1842. His wife was a member of the wealthy Usher family of Edinburgh and was said to have married considerably below her station. How did such a woman, accustomed to ladylike pursuits only, adapt to life in a log shanty in solid bush where supplies had to be brought in by water because there were no roads?

The Lunns lived here and worked at clearing the land for ten years until Lord Elgin, Governor General of Upper and Lower Canada appointed him chairman of the building committee for the jail and courthouse in Owen Sound. He was then appointed the first Registrar of Grey County and served as Mayor of Owen Sound for two terms from 1862.

James Ross bought the property for £650 in 1860 from Thomas Lunn. The house is characterized by the ell shape — a configuration of some practicality. It presents its strictly formal facade to the community while the addition to the rear provided a sheltered entrance. As time went on these tails grew longer with perhaps a woodshed, a driving shed, a pumphouse tacked on behind. The stone for the front facade is said to have been found on the shore in one piece. It was broken and then transported by horse and wagon to the building site.

THE ROBERT ELLIOT HOUSE - "MAPLESTONE" c.1855

Sydenham Township Lot 38 Con B

ROBERT ELLIOT (1810-1894) was born near Ettrick in Dumfries-shire, Scotland. In his youth he was a retainer on the estate of the Duke of Buccleugh, a member of the Scottish lowland's titled aristocracy. Elliot came to Galt, Canada in 1837 and up to Sydenham in 1843 to claim a grant of fifty acres from the Crown. Here his large family of sons was born and raised and here he cleared the land, built his stone house and farmed — until his death at the age of eighty-four.

Most of the first settlers of Sydenham engaged in heavy physical labour all of their lives, raised large families, were pillars of the church and active in community life. Almost to a man they lived to a great old age. This is not so true of the women.

Elliot's house is a modest one-and-a-half-storey stone cottage, built to shelter the generations. There is nothing shoddy about the materials or inappropriate about the design. The house stands as a concise statement of a family and a culture.

TOWN OF THORNBURY

c.1890

Thornbury 21 Bruce St. N. (Plan 1023 Lot 83 — Thornbury Mill Site Block.)

THE THORNBURY "mill site" block of land (seventy-one acres) was granted by the Crown to the Honorable William Beverly Robinson in 1854. He was one of Upper Canada's wealthiest and most influential citizens. Here is a prime example of the collusion between the Crown and the Family Compact in the handing out of free land without any residency requirements. Obviously, the Honorable Robinson had no intention of moving from the town of York to the shore of Georgian Bay in the deep wilderness to build a mill and to live there. He did intend, though, to profit from the deal with the Crown by selling the "mill site" to another wealthy and influential citizen of Owen Sound, Judge Wilkes, who did build a mill which his estate leased to a succession of millers. The building lots were sold by his widow, Ann. In 1891 lots 5 and 6 were sold to John Dickinson for one thousand dollars. He was likely the builder of this Gothic Revival house.

The ell-shaped house presents a picturesque facade to the street. The entrance is well composed with its glazed transom and sidelights and is surmounted with the same Tudor style labels as the bay windows. Slender posts with delicate brackets support the verandah roof which shelters the second front entrance.

GLOSSARY

ASHLAR Stone that has been cut square and dressed.

BAY A window, door, or other opening, comprising one division of a facade.

CORNICE The projecting horizontal element at the intersection of the exterior wall and the roof.

DENTIL A small, tooth-like square block, used in a row as a decorative feature in a cornice.

DORMER A window that projects from a sloping roof with a small roof of its own.

ELL Refers to the "L" shape of a structure.

ENTABLATURE The horizontal component that lies directly above a column or a wall.

FRIEZE A wide horizontal band at the top of an exterior wall.

GABLE The triangular upper portion of a wall at the roofline.

GEORGIAN STYLE Named after the English monarchs of the 18th and early 19th century, modeled on the ruins of Greek and Roman Classical buildings and revived in 18th century Europe.

GOTHIC REVIVAL STYLE Refers to a late 18th and 19th century revival of the picturesque medieval architecture of England, France and other western European countries.

ITALIANATE STYLE Derived from the villa architecture of Tuscany, Italy.

LABEL A rectangular moulding to throw off the rain above a window or door.

LINTEL The horizontal supporting member at the top of a door or window.

LUG SILL The lower horizontal member which extends beyond the vertical sides of a window frame, as opposed to a "slip sill" which is flush.

NEO-CLASSIC STYLE Inspired from the architectural remains of ancient Greece and Rome, popular in Canada from about the 1820's until about 1860.

OCULUS A circular opening in a wall.

PALLADIAN STYLE Derived from the buildings and publications of the Italian architect of the 16th century, Andrea Palladio.

QUOIN Squared members at the corner of a wall, usually laid alternately with small and large faces. May be structural or decorative.

REGENCY COTTAGE A ground-hugging, square, hip-roofed structure with a centre hall plan.

SECOND EMPIRE STYLE Most easily recognized by the Mansard or broken roof combined with a rich classicizing treatment of the facade.

SIDELIGHT A window beside a door, forming part of the door unit.

TEE Refers to the "T" shape of a structure.

TRANSOM A window above a door, forming part of the door unit.

TREILLAGE A decorative latticework support used in verandahs and constructed of wood or metal.

VOUSSOIR A brick or wedge-shaped stone forming one of the units of an arch. The central voussoir is the keystone.

Bibliography

GENERAL INTEREST

Adamson, Anthony and Willard, John, *The Gaiety Of Gables,* McClelland and Stewart, 1974

Akenson, Donald Harmon, *The Irish In Ontario — A Study In Rural History,* McGill-Queen's University Press, 1984

Arnot, D.H., *Gothic Architecture Applied To Modern Residences,* New York, 1851

Blake, V.B.B. and Greenhill, Ralph, *Rural Ontario,* University of Toronto Press, 1969

Brand, Stewart, *How Buildings Learn — What Happens After They're Built,* Viking-Penquin, 1994

Brosseau, Mathilde, *The Neo-Gothic Style In Canadian Architecture,* Canadian Historic Sites: Occasional Papers in Archaeology and History No 25, 1980

Byers, Mary and McBurney, Margaret, *Atlantic Hearth — Early Homes And Families Of Nova Scotia,* University of Toronto Press, 1994

Cameron, Christina and Wright, Janet, *The Second Empire Style In Canadian Architecture,* Canadian Historical Sites: Occcasional Papers in Archaeology and History No. 24

Clerk, Nathalie, *Palladian Style In Canadian Architecture, Research Publications,* Parks Canada, Ottawa, 19849

Downing, A.J., *The Architecture Of Country Houses, Including Designs For Cottages, Farm Houses And Villas,* New York, 1850

Gillon Jr., Edmond V. and Lancaster, Clay, *Victorian Houses, A Treasury Of Lesser-Known Examples,* Dover reprint, New York, 1973

Greenhill, Ralph and MacPherson, Ken and Richardson, Douglas, *Ontario Towns,* Oberon, 1975

Hussey, E.C., *Cottage Architecture Of Victorian America,* Dover reprint, New York, 1994

Jacques, D.H., *The House : A Manual Of Rural Architecture,* New York, 1868

Kalman, Harold, A *History Of Canadian Archtecture Vol I, Vol II,* Oxford University Press, Toronto, 1994

Loudon, J.C., *Encyclopedia Of Cottage, Farm And Villa Architecture And Furniture,* London, 1833

MacRae, Marion and Adamson, Anthony, *The Ancestral Roof — Domestic Architecture In Upper Canada,* Clarke Irwin, Toronto, 1963

Maitland, Leslie, *Neoclassical Architecture In Canada,* Research Publications, Parks Canada, Ottawa, 1984

Nuttgens, Patrick, *The Story Of Architecture,* Phaidon Press, London, 1983

Ondaatje, Kim and Mackenzie, Lois, *Old Ontario Houses,* Gage, Toronto, 1977

Rempel, John I., *Building With Wood And Other Aspects Of 19th Century Building In Central Canada*, Revised Edition, University of Toronto Press, 1980

Richardson, C.J., *Picturesque Designs For Mansions, Villas, Lodges Etc.,* London, 1870

Ritchie, T., *Canada Builds 1867-1967,* University of Toronto Press, 1967

The Local History Collection in the Owen Sound Public Library

The Township Histories of Grey County have been a valuable aid in the research into the houses and their families in this volume. The pioneer families who provided the basic material, the working committees and their editors are all to be congratulated for their important and, in some cases, lyrical work. Because these histories are the product of so many individuals rather than one or two authors, I have chosen to list the following by title alphabetically.

Beautiful Stoney Keppel, Including The Village Of Shallow Lake 1855-1986

Brooke, Beattie, Walter & Graham, Ed. Croft, Melba

County Of Grey Directory, W. W. SMITH 1865, Owen Sound, 1865

Emigration : The British Farmer's And Farm Labourer's Guide To Ontario, The Premier Province Of The Dominion Of Canada, Toronto, 1880

Early Settlement And Development Of Collingwood Township, Rorke, Major Edward

The Early Days Of Owen Sound, A. M. Stephens

Eminent Women Of Grey County, Grey County Historical Society, Ed. Coke, Sharon

Euphrasia — Glimpses Past And Present, 1989

Fourth Entrance To Huronia, Croft, Melba, 1980

From Quill To Ballpoint 1591-1988, Vick, Dorothy, 1988

Grey County's 125th Year — 1852-1977 — A Brief History Of The Municipalities Of Grey County, Rutherford, A.M. and Bravener, M.

A History Of Bentinck Township, 1978

A History Of The County Of Grey, Marsh, E.L., Owen Sound, 1931

History Of Derby Township 1839-1972

A History Of Glenelg Township, 1985

The History Of Sullivan Township 1850-1975

History Of Sydenham Township, 1967

A History Of The Town Of Durham 1842-1994

Historical Atlas Of Grey And Bruce Counties, H. Belden & Co., 1880

Home Words, Stories About The People And Places Of Owen Sound, Armitage, Andrew, Ginger Press, 1987

Houses In South East Grey: A Study Of History And Architecture, Brownridge, Jean

An Illustrated History Of Collingwood Township, 1979

The Legal And Commercial Exchange (Mercantile Agency) Of Canada, January 1884

Markdale — The Crossroads Of Grey, 1988

Markdale And Flesherton — A Written Heritage, 1979

Normanby Reflections — A History Of Normanby Township, 1989

Mer Douce, Volume I, The Story Of Ontario, The Algonquin Historical Society, 1921-23

Owen Sound On The Georgian Bay Canada 1912, Reesor, Emma B. Buchan and Thomson, Norah

Owen Sound: The Day The Governor General Came To Town & Other Tales, Armitage Andrew, Boston Mills Press, 1979

Owen Sound : Steamboat Days, Armitage, Andrew, Boston Mills Press, 1981

The Paths That Led To Holland, Volume I 1983, *Volume II* 1990

Peace, Plenty And Progress — A History Of Osprey Township, 1975

The People Of Owen Sound, Croft, Melba

The Poetical Directory Of Owen Sound, 1863

Priceville And Its Roots — Routes, 1992

Reminiscences Of North Sydenham, An Historical Sketch Of Annan And Leith, Ross, Allan, Owen Sound 1924, second edition 1991

Split Rail Country: A History Of Artemesia Township, 1986

Township Of Proton 1857-1982 An Historical Sketch

Vetting The Vernacular — Ontario History, Volume 74, number 2, pages 66-94

While We Still Remember — A History Of Egremont 1840-1983

William Armstrong And His Descendants 1846-1976 Pioneer Of Markdale, Ontario, Editors: Armstrong, Herbert K. and Phyllis E.